Road to the Crown

with Trinity Bush

All Rights Reserved

Copyright © 2021

Beyond What You See, LLC

Produced, Published by
Raising A Mogul, LLC/Zandra Brand Publishing

Edited by Terri King Hunt, Superior Guidance, LLC

No part of this book may be reproduced, stored in a retrieval system, or transmitted, in any form or by any means written, electronic, recording, or photocopying without the written permission of the creator Beyond What You See, LLC

Printed in the United States of America
First Printing, 2021

ISBN 978-1-7372752-0-6

Books may be purchased via

www.BeyondWhatYouSee.net

TABLE OF CONTENTS

Introduction vii

Forward xv

Chapter 1: The Fall That Brought Me the Win 1

Chapter 2: Try Until You Win 7

Chapter 3: Practice Makes Progress 13

Chapter 4: My Story Matters 19

Chapter 5: It's a Fun Ride! 25

Chapter 6: Unleash Your Superpower 37

Chapter 7: The Twins who chase their dreams 43

Chapter 8: A Natural Crown 49

Chapter 9: From nonverbal to speaking on a national stage! 55

Chapter 10: It's So Much Bigger Than a Crown 61

Chapter 11: My First Big Win 67

Chapter 12: The Power of… 73

Chapter 13: The Direct and Changing Path 81

Chapter 14: Dreams They Do Come True 87

Chapter 15: Uniquely Me! 95

Meet the Authors 103

Road to the Crown with Trinity Bush

I might be small but
I WILL make a huge impact
—Trinity Bush

Road to the Crown with Trinity Bush

INTRODUCTION

What are your first thoughts when you hear the word pageant? Do you think of fake hair, glitz and glamour, self-absorbed women, makeup, and false teeth? When I think of the word pageant I think of confidence, poise, public speaking, elegance, and girl power. I think of sweaty hands, scattered words, intensity to win, laughter, anxiousness, and support.

In my 3 years of pageants, you would be surprised to know that although I have held 2 pageant titles, my parents were completely against my participation in pageants. For years people would admire my personality and comment on how perfect it was for the pageant world. They would encourage my parents to put me in pageants but they were not having it. To their credit, they shared the common misconceptions that many people have. All they could imagine was catty kids, heavy makeup, competitive and cruel moms, and every other negative thing that has been highlighted in reality TV.

In spite of their fears, they decided to give it a chance and 3 years later I, Trinity Bush, have found my "happy place" right here in the world of pageantry. While pageantry has become my first love, there are so many other things that also make me happy. I am a 10-year-old pageant queen but I am also the CEO of Beyond What You See, a company I founded in 2020. I am a Best Selling Author of an anthology titled The Science Behind It. I am a model, keynote speaker, influencer, dancer, and actress. I bounce around in many worlds but pageantry is the one thing that combines all of my interests in one place!

The physical CROWN is the first attraction at a pageant, it is full of diamonds and rhinestones and is usually absolutely beautiful. Whenever I register for a new pageant I always check out what the crown looks like on the registration website. It is not what is most important but, I am always interested in what it looks like. Over the years I have come to understand that pageantry is not only about a tangible crown, it is also about an intangible CROWN.

To earn the crown you must be

C- COURAGEOUS

R- RESILIENT

O- OPEN-HEARTED

W- a WINNER

N- NIFTY

In anything you do, there is a crown, an ultimate prize. In basketball the "crown" is the championship trophy, in gymnastics, it's a gold medal in football it's a Heisman trophy and in school,

Introduction

it's an "A". Regardless of the "crown" you're after, you can use these CROWN pillars to achieve it. If you want to be successful you must be Courageous, Resilient, and Open-Hearted. You must have the heart of a Winner as well as a Nifty mind.

When you are courageous you're not deterred by danger or pain. To achieve your goal you must be brave. My most brave pageant moment was in November 2020 at a National pageant. I dream about it often. Not because I placed 1st winner up, not because it was the biggest pageant of my experience, not even because I was wearing the most beautiful custom-made gown by my favorite designer Bryan K. Osburn but because I wore COURAGE like a badge of honor all week! I made a decision at the beginning of the pageant week that I would walk into every event not deterred by my own fear. That I was going to feel the fear but do it anyway. This is a skill we must all develop if we want to achieve greatness. Imagine if every time you got scared, you quit; you gave up; you stopped trying. Would you ever accomplish anything? The answer is no because Fear is ALWAYS present. So you must learn to be Courageous.

You have to be Resilient. Able to withstand or recover quickly from difficult conditions. According to my parents, I have been talking since I came out of my mom's belly. I am a talker, a laugher, a very dramatic and passionate girl. I have always had a unique way in which I care for others and desire to see others happy and feeling good! So, it only made sense that I follow in my mom's footsteps and start my own business. In March of 2020, I started a business called Beyond What You See, where we encourage, motivate and empower kids to embrace their perfect imperfections through public speaking and self-esteem fashion shows. Literally, 2 weeks after starting my business, the world shut down due to the coronavirus. This forced us all into quarantine. I instantly thought, "What a waste of time. I put so much work into starting my business and now I can't even be face to face with people to help them." During that time, I began participating in a virtual kids' business school called Young Mogul Prep School. Later that week after class I told my teachers that my feelings were hurt and that I wasted my time. One of them said, "Trinity you don't have to stop building your business, you just need to pivot and adjust." Pivot? I didn't even know what that word meant!

I remember my mom and I talked for days about this. My feelings were hurt and I just felt sad. Then it hit me, there are other ways to reach people and improve their self-esteem. I came up with the idea to make audio affirmations and affirmation t-shirts. Those things can be shared virtually and can still help others to love themselves! My dad told me I acted resiliently before I even knew how to spell the word! Lol, When was your last pivot moment? How were you resilient? How did you recover, withstand or get through the situation?

To win you have to be Open-Hearted: honest and open to all possibilities. I will admit before pageantry I was sometimes a sore

Introduction

loser. I believed that if you competed in something, winning was the only option. I learned from my pageant coach that this mindset was really closed and would keep me from seeing other possibilities. We have to get comfortable with the idea that all of the wins we experience are not "THE WIN." When I learned to open my heart I was able to see endless possibilities in every situation, meaning I was able to learn life lessons from every 2nd place, 10th place, and no place.

You have to be a Winner: a person or thing that wins something. This definition may be weird here because I just talked about not making winning the most important thing. My parents were intentional about having a village of people around so that I can get many perspectives in my life. Adults around me are always giving me advice and helping me to be better. Sometimes it's annoying but most times I'm okay with it. I can't remember who told me this but a winner is someone who learns from their mistakes and applies them to their life. In doing this, they always win. I really like this statement and have actually used it in school. For example, if you take a spelling test and you miss half of the questions or only earn a 60%, the next time you take a spelling test you use that 60% to help you get a higher score. Change up your study plan, eat peppermint or play certain music softly, just make sure you learn from your mistakes by doing things differently the second time around.

Finally, you have to be Nifty: skillful and resourceful. Backstage during pageants are the BEST! Moms turn into the most resourceful scientists! Lol, There are safety pins, bobby pins, magnets, steamers, tissues in the backs of shoes, holes being sewn up, hemming tape and everything in between. For most pageants I begin to prepare at least 8 weeks in advance but I have learned that no matter how long you prepare or how much you prepare, hiccups will always happen! I remember my very first national pageant, I was clear across the country in California. My mom bought me the cutest nude heels and I was so excited to wear them. We were on break and decided to leave the hotel to find snacks. Since my heels were new I wanted to get some practice walking in them so I decided to wear them on our walk. I was running down the sidewalk and having so much fun when suddenly my heel broke off! I was devastated and began to cry because these were my shoes for my formal gown. My mom stopped inside a Walgreens and grabbed some super glue. She instantly turned into Superwoman and before I knew it we were sitting on the sidewalk and she was fixing my shoes. That is what I call nifty!! Being resourceful is necessary because things happen in every situation no matter how prepared you are. Are you resourceful?

These 5 standards are sometimes hard for us kids to operate in but hard doesn't mean impossible. I wanted to write this book to help other kids "win at life" while using these standards. I want my peers to know that when adults tell us "nothing is impossible" they

Introduction

are telling the truth! We just need to turn on our power and operate within these standards and see the possibilities for ourselves.

I found 14 young ladies who all possess courage, resilience, are open-hearted, are winners and are extremely nifty. I found my tribe, my group, girls just like me. Girls, who love wearing heels but also will trade them in for some tennis shoes to play a game of kickball. Girls, who have taken the life lessons learned through pageantry and applied them to their lives so that they win in all areas. Girls who know wearing a sash and crown means nothing without integrity, values and serving others. Girls, who are willingly to help each other and willingly accept help.

These 14 ladies are going to take you on a fun journey through their experiences of highs, lows, titles and losses, tears of sadness and tears of joy as well. I hope this book helps you build self confidence and make you more comfortable in your skin.

This book will inspire you, motivate you and take you on many of the same emotions as the authors. I can't wait for you to learn that pageantry is BEYOND WHAT YOU SEE!

~ **Trinity Amanda Nicole Bush,**
Pageant Queen, CEO, Keynote Speaker,
Model, Actress & Affirmation Slanger

Road to the Crown with Trinity Bush

FORWARD

Even before I won my first National Title, it was easy to see how pageantry was changing the lives of young women and families everywhere. Once the crown sat upon my head, it became crystal clear that my passion was changing the lives of the future women of our society.

It is breathtaking to believe that thousands upon thousands of girls across the country, who may have never met each other in person, have established an undoubtedly incredible connection with each other without even realizing it. Even more amazing for most people is that those thousands of girls consist of like-minded young women who are striving to change the world - otherwise known as "Pageant Girls." Trinity, myself, and the 14 other young authors of this book are a part of this remarkable sisterhood.

Something very unique about *Road to The Crown* is that there are 15 different perspectives of what pageantry truly is. Nevertheless, they all agree, pageantry sets you on the road to success. My journey from taking a seat in the back of the classroom to gracing the National stage with the words "National

American Miss Jr. Teen" across my chest has been one of a long six years. But it has been the most rewarding experience of my life.

This book holds the treasured stories of young women close to achieving their goals like winning their National titles and young women who have reached their goals and are now shooting for the stars. I can assure you that these stories will encourage you to stay confident in yourself and true to the journey God has given you.

~ **Arica Haywood**
2020-2021 National American Miss Jr. Teen

FORWARD

Pageantry is more than a crown and banner. Yes, it's fantastic to have that beautiful crown, but you will soon learn that it is so much more. The young girls in this book share the experiences and lessons they are learning from competing in pageants whether it be life-long skills like public speaking, how they are making a difference in the community, or overall how pageantry has been beneficial to them. I know that pageants have changed my life just like it is for them.

I met Trinity a few years ago after seeing her compete in a pageant that I had once competed in at the same age. In Trinity, I saw a special girl with a bright future. She didn't walk away as the winner of that pageant, but I reached out to encourage her not to give up because I knew her time would come. She didn't give up, and her time did come that next year when she walked away as Miss North Carolina Junior Pre-Teen. Now she is publishing her own book! How amazing is that? This is just some of what pageants do. They encourage girls to dream big and to accomplish their dreams. To Trinity and pageant girls everywhere, keep making a difference and reaching for the stars! Congrats to girls in this book for being featured and sharing your experiences in pageantry! I'm honored to introduce these girls because they are accomplishing so much at a young age and truly are inspiring.

~ **Alexandria Palmer**
International United Miss Connecticut 2021

Chapter 1
THE FALL THAT BROUGHT ME THE WIN
JURNEE BUSH

*A girl can be anything she wants to be
and I've decided to be EVERYTHING*
~Jurnee Bush

Announcer: Jurnee, your on-stage question is, what did you learn by doing this pageant?

Me: I learned the Queens Rules and they are: heads up, shoulders back, hands by your side, smile, and be confident.

I was the kid that talked to no one outside my family. The kid that would hide behind my parent's legs when others would try to talk to me. Sometimes I was brave enough to talk to my peers but I was never brave enough to talk to adults…..never! That day when I recited the queen's rule, a new ME was born.

That new me is Jurnee. That's right my name is Jurnee Bush and I am 8 years old from Charlotte, North Carolina. I love gymnastics and am really good at it. I love hanging out with my sisters, singing, dancing, and oh yeah….anything my big sister Trinity is into.

The pageant described above was actually my 2nd pageant. My first pageant was the perfect beginner experience. The first pageant prepared me for the second. It was the first time I had ever spoken alone to several unfamiliar adults. That process is called an interview, it is the portion of the pageant where each contestant rotates individually to each judge to answer impromptu questions. The questions are very thought-provoking. Sometimes I gave great answers, sometimes I didn't even know what to say and others I knew what to say but was too scared to say it. The judges were so sweet and patient with each of us. When I froze one just nodded at me and said I was doing fine. I didn't win the first pageant I was in but I won life lessons for sure!

My parents always taught me to never give up. Before we could even make it home from that first pageant, I told my parents that I wanted to compete again the following year. My momma always says we are the most ambitious girls in the world. I guess she is right because for the remainder of that year I juggled 2nd grade, 12 hours of gymnastics, and pageant practice. Speaking of my momma's girls, I am the baby of my sisters. There are 3 of us.

The Fall That Brought Me the Win

My 1st-grade year was awesome! I came into school ready to make new friends and have more playdates! I'm pretty sure I made friends with everyone in the class that year. There was no point in going back in my shell, I had come all out at the pageant. Now, I still wasn't fond of adults, but pageantry definitely opened me up socially in ways my parents couldn't even imagine.

After a year of working on gymnastics and in between preparing for the next Carolina's Girls Rock Pageant, it was almost time to compete. I helped my mom pick out my outfits and loved the preparation. We would look up YouTube videos to find hairstyles and I helped her design my bling outfit for the blue jean bling optional. My mom is the queen of "hand me downs," so of course my pageant gown was a beautiful dress my big sister had worn in a previous pageant. A typical Friday night for us would be pageant practice followed by family games. I would be sitting in a chair in the middle of the living room and my parents and sisters would be sitting on the couches. They would take turns asking me potential questions that the judges might ask, and I would practice my public speaking. My dad would always tell me that he was less concerned with me winning but more concerned with me gaining confidence in my speaking. The night before the pageant was a blur but the day of the pageant I will never forget.

I got up that morning and had a big breakfast to include my favorite strawberry oatmeal and bacon! My sisters were my biggest cheerleaders that day! Kylah is the oldest and at the time she was

17, in the middle is Trinity who was 8, and at the time I was 6 years old. They were definitely my hype girls that morning and we sang and danced all morning!!

I remember the pageant like it was yesterday. I arrived with my family all cheering behind me, I had the cutest outfits in my bag, my hair looked like an African queen and my confidence was through the roof!! Every time I was on stage, my confidence was coming out of my skin! My favorite part of the pageant was the optional, Bling Runway. Not only was I cute, but I modeled my outfit like a New York Runway model! Oh and I can't forget about the opening number dance, I had so much fun with that too!

My momma always tells my sisters and me that challenges always come with success. That day was not lacking in challenges just because it was amazing. It was a day of my highest highs and most embarrassing lows. I made it through the entire pageant and was proud of myself at every part of the process. The judges had turned in their scores and, praise God, because I don't know if what happened next would have changed the scores. Lol

All of the girls were doing the final walk on the stage before the winners were announced. I had done my walk at the front of the stage and was making my full circle by walking off the stage in the back and "boom", I fell off the back of the stage. I was in pain from the fall but more than anything I was embarrassed. My family ran to the back of the stage and all of the staff. They picked me up,

The Fall That Brought Me the Win

comforted me, and consoled me. The Director of the pageant delayed the pageant for about 20 mins to ensure I was okay. Finally, I got myself together and was ready to complete the pageant. We took our places on stage and got ready to hear the winners.

All I remember at that point was hearing "the 2019 Carolina Girl's Rock Princess is Jurnee Bush!!!!!" My heart was racing, and my body was ready to explode with excitement! I was proud of myself for speaking during the interviews, proud of myself for walking the stage with confidence, proud of myself for pushing myself to compete again, and for coming back from the most embarrassing moment of my life.

My parents were proud, my sisters were proud and most importantly I was proud. Nothing was the same after that day. My year of reign was full of volunteer work for the homeless in the school system, volunteering at different events to help people, and showing up to appearances. I knew my year of reign was only for a year, but my mom always taught me that I was a queen before the sash and crown and I will remain a queen even after I hand down the sash and crown.

My road to the crown taught me self-confidence and how to build my self-esteem. I loved doing those two pageants. I still live by the Queen's Rules today! I was so shy before pageants, but I am a lot more open now! I don't feel as scared anymore to talk to people or to have the spotlight on me. The lessons I learned from pageantry have helped in gymnastics and in school. As of right now, I've put the pageant heels aside so that I can rock super cute leotards and master my floor routines as a gymnast. My road to the crown has become my road to life! Will I ever do a pageant again? I don't know but what I do know is that I have convinced myself that I am able to do anything I put my mind to!

Chapter 2
TRY UNTIL YOU WIN
ZARIA MARTIN RILEY

*"Beauty begins the moment
you decide to be yourself"*
~Coco Chanel

You know the saying, if at first, you don't succeed, try until you WIN!! Oh wait, that's my saying but, ultimately, I had to try and try again. I can still hear my moms' voice in my head, "You got this Pickle, I love you", I believe those words among many others helped me to place 2nd runner up in the 2018 pageant system I participated in.

Neither my mother nor myself were familiar with pageantry prior to receiving my very first piece of mail from a national pageant system. I was only 6 years old, yet the letter was an invitation to interview for their National Pageant. It seemed easy enough once I discovered the curiosity and excitement my mother displayed. Upon arriving I saw girls of many different ages, schools (including one from mine), and many different ethnicities and because of this, we had no idea what to expect. We were greeted by the State Queens in each division and I remember my first thought, "I want a crown like that".

A few more meetings, mailings, and months passed and we still had no real idea of what was in store, but I was registered to participate. Then it happened on check-in day. Once on the property, I saw some of the girls I befriended at the initial events but there were so many more. The first day was a lot to take in. In fact, the whole weekend was. With so many things going on in 1 weekend it felt like it was much longer.

What I remember most about August 2018 is that I won NOTHING but I looked pretty. I knew I wanted a crown but didn't understand the time, energy, and talent that it represented. I met a friend that weekend that became a lifelong pageant sister. It was her first year as well. We promised to cheer each other on and she placed 2nd runner up!! When they called her up I was nervous, excited, and sad at the same time. Sad because I didn't win anything and because I didn't know if I would see her again. Nervous and excited because she was being called to the stage in front of a room full of people. Both of our moms were cheering, but I sat quietly trying to understand what was happening and how I felt about it all. My mother noticed how quiet I had become and attempted to cheer me up by taking pictures and telling me what a great job I had done. The only thing I could think of after learning that my friend was going to Nationals and had a crown was that I needed to get my own.

After all of the pictures and dinner with my family, my mother and I had "the talk". We talked about sportsmanship and support. She asked me if I enjoyed pageantry and I told her I did. I told her that I really wanted to do it again and she agreed to help me be my best. My mother found a coach who was the best of the best in Washington, DC; Ms. J Kelly of Talent 4 Kids. Next thing I knew we were signed and committed to training. My mommy, my twin, and I drove 1 hour every Saturday for pageant and modeling training. Ms. Kelly had trained a lot of girls in my area that went on to win crowns at National levels. It was a lot of work but it was worth it.

The experience of becoming a trained model has helped me to land many opportunities outside of the pageant circuit. My mother told me she believed I could but she needed me to believe I could do it. Once I told her I wanted it and would try that was all she needed to get things moving. I understand that this came with a lot of sacrifice for both my family and myself. For me because I love to sleep but, my family also made sacrifices for me. All I can say is it wasn't fruitless.

August 2019 I WAS READY!! Being the youngest in my coaching class came with its advantages. I got to hear about all of the other girls' victories *and* trials within different pageant systems, learn about wardrobe fails, etiquette and work extra hard at my absolute new favorite thing, MODELING. Check-in was smoother and although I was just a year older, I was a year wiser and it made a great difference. My mother handed me my portfolio and it began.

I went from table to table introducing myself and getting my itinerary, number, and directions for things to come. Not knowing who was the scariest part of all. Here's a freebie tidbit for ya, you won't know who the judges are until the very end so remember to be you, be beautiful, and be polite in every encounter because someone is always watching. Thinking back, I felt a bit empowered, a bit "teenagerish" if you will, my mother bringing up the rear and with me just being me and being allowed to speak for myself and answer questions.

As the weekend passed, I became more and more acquainted with my pageant sisters while meeting new ones. Having fun, exchanging journeys, talking, taking selfies, and complimenting each other on the various talents displayed. This weekend didn't feel half as long as the year before. They say time flies when you're having lots of fun and it sure did. Even my mother seemed more relaxed and having more fun this year with the pageant moms she met.

The night of the finale finally arrived. All of the months of practice would definitely show to someone and if not, at least I knew how hard I had worked. I last saw my mother before she took her seat after the opening dance. Her last words to me were "You got this, I love you Pickle" as I fluffed out my dress waving to her reassuring her that I remembered all of the talks we had leading up to this moment and that I knew I would always be a winner to her.

My resume was not completed until we arrived at the hotel but my mother said "this is all you boo" and literally read the questions off to me as I stood beside her. She wrote my answers verbatim without even taking a picture of it for memory's sake but, guess what, I WON IT!! That's right, I won Best Resume in the Princess Division. My Casual Wear Modeling outfit was not an original but, guess what, I WALKED THE STAGE and WON!! The Top Model Search outfit was definitely something that I felt my brightest self in and could later be used as a school outfit. I took that category too!!! 2nd Runner Up was the furthest from my mind after being called up to the stage for the previous categories.

In my mind, I *HAD WON* even before they called the winner. I believed in what I was doing and stayed the course of training. It was what I wanted and more importantly continued to tell myself I could do. I could win *something*!! I returned back to my seat after the final category. As they began to call the Queen's Court I realized I was tearing up again. I wasn't sure why I was so emotional but, I was having that same nervous and excited feeling again. After winning all of the trophies, I realized we were now at the moment of truth. They called my name as one of the top 5 in the Queen's Court after the emcee looked down and caught a glance of me teary-eyed and my now quiet mommy! My mother and I both jumped up and I ran as quickly as I could, tripping up the stairs. This meant that not only was I going to California but that I had a chance for the crown.

On stage, there were so many feelings inside me. My tummy was doing flips over the moments to come. If I would win against one of my newly found pageant sisters that would mean she would be crowning me and losing her title but, even if I lost, I would be going home this year with something to show for it. At that moment I understood my emotionalness, the reason for my tears. I was proud of myself, the many days of missed sleep, the goals set for myself, and more importantly, new skills and a world of opportunity waiting.

When I started pageantry, I had no idea it even existed but, after starting I didn't want the fun to end. It is a sisterhood like no other. You begin as strangers with nothing in common except participation but through making friends and teaching each other you find sisters for life. We made up dances, jokes, shared stories and even the moms formed bonds through travel that none of us will ever forget. I'm just glad that I wasn't afraid to continue to believe in the invisible crown on my head until I got the real one by working hard and never giving up.

Chapter 3
PRACTICE MAKES PROGRESS
JAZMINE PALMA

"Courage, sacrifice, determination, commitment, toughness, heart, talent, guts. That's what little girls are made of; the heck with sugar and spice."
~Bethany Hamilton

Supreme Court Justice Sonia Sotomayor once said "The Latina in me is an ember that blazes forever". It is the Latina in me that gives me the strength to keep pushing forward even when it seems like everything is going wrong.

Hola mi nombre es Jazmine Palma I am the 2020 North Carolina National American Miss Jr Preteen. While holding this title is one of my biggest accomplishments to date. Getting here was no easy task and the road to my crown was filled with many mistakes and many embarrassing moments.

This is the story of My Road to the Crown.

I began doing pageants in 2017. It was a school pageant and all my friends were joining. I didn't know much about pageants but I knew I wanted to participate so I asked my mom if I could join and she said yes. I was so excited! When the big practice day came the coaches were teaching us how to walk and do stances and I was just trying to figure out what I would be doing on the day of the pageant. Even though I had no idea what I was doing, I was a natural. I finished that school pageant and was crowned the winner. I had my first crown and sash. I was hooked. I knew that day that I wanted to do more pageants. My mom and dad watched me and agreed, they saw how much I enjoyed the experience, so my mom began researching the world of pageants.

My mom learned that there are many types of pageants and the ones she wanted for me were the all-natural pageants. She started looking for local, all-natural pageants and soon discovered one pageant system that was all-natural and taught their participants "how" to be a queen. The director was serious, she had staff who taught me to: Walk with my head held high, speak clearly, and much, much more. That local pageant was the biggest pageant I had been in and had some much fun. We learned so much about ourselves and others. More importantly, we had fun learning this craft. That pageant director became my pageant coach, Ms. Donna Murrell, my pageant coach is passionate about the pageant world which shows in her teaching.

Practice Makes Progress

In my first pageant with her as my coach, I competed against 14 girls. We went to practice and learned how to walk. I learned about her, "Queens Rules". Her rules really helped me do well in her pageants and other pageants as well. We went to weekly practices where she had different styles and forms that taught me confidence, poise, self-love, and other techniques that got me where I am today. Well in that first pageant weekend, the director planned the weekend for us to go to the Mall and walked around waving and greeting other people. I got to have so much fun with all my new friends that I had made over the weeks of training. When it was time to do the pageant and talk to the judges in the interview, I was amazingly comfortable talking to them. They made me feel like I was especially important, and they wanted to learn more about me. Then it was stage time, I was nervous but had more fun than I thought I would. I got 4th runner up and Ms. Photogenic. It was amazing.

I was on a mission to get better and I just knew it was going to happen. That is when I experienced the most embarrassing moment of my pageant journey. I was getting prepared to go backstage and I pulled my dress down a little bit too hard and I ended up RIPPING MY DRESS. I was so scared because we didn't have a backup dress that would match the shoes I was wearing. I was panicking. When my mom finally got me to calm down she suggested we simply tuck the ripped part of my dress under the belt and go on as if nothing had happened. As I started to walk on stage, she warned me not to move too much or it might come undone. I was second in line and was super scared to go on the stage because I feared that while I was walking something bad would happen

I made it all the way across the stage and was just about to walk off stage when the unthinkable happened. My sash fell to my feet and just as I bent over to gracefully pick it up, my tucked dress fell down also. I was so embarrassed, but I kept it together and walked off the stage with poise and grace.

After that, I did about 3 more pageants with my coach, and each time I did one, I learned something new and different. I had so much fun, I started thinking of Donna and her staff as family. One day, Ms. Donna suggested I consider doing other pageants with other organizations. I tried pageants with other organizations and did really well. In one, I competed against 50 girls at my state level. In that pageant, I met people from other cities in North Carolina. I even got to have fun in the top model part.

That is where I got my picture taken by a professional photographer, they would tell me to turn, jump, and just have fun so I did. That was a fun weekend. Now, I didn't like it when I was on stage with the top 5 and the other girls were hitting each other with their roses. I just stood there thinking, "OMG, please leave me alone!" "I am listening for my name." The other girls left one by one. As I stood there with the other girl, she started hitting me with her Rose. In that pageant, I placed 1st runner up in my division, Top Model, and 1 runner up in Casual Wear. I was so proud of myself and to see my mom and coach look like I was a queen and that made me feel happy, but I wasn't settling for 1st runner up and went back and did more because I wanted the crown. I wasn't stopping until I got my crown.

Then in 2020, I participated in one of my biggest pageants so far. The weekend was amazing and I was focused. I met a lot of new friends and worked really hard to represent myself well. The hard work, determination, and embarrassment of previous pageants all paid off because as we all stood on the stage and I listened for my name I heard "and the winner is Jazmine Palma". The win was indescribable and the best part was my friend Trinity Bush got to crown me as her successor.

Since I have started pageants, I have been in 2 school plays, photoshoots, won places in runway events, and other activities that require public speaking. I have 2 crowns, sashes, and lots of trophies.

Out of all this experience, I have really learned what I want to be when I grow up and it may change, but for now, I want to be a family law attorney. I want to help kids that are being abused, no food, or someone who needs help and has no voice. I want to be a voice for them. For now, I am only 10 years old, I had more opportunities than I ever had or would have had. Challenges may come and go, but my pageant families and friends, we will be there for one another. There are more things to learn in this world (pageant and life), one step at a time we will make a difference, and I choose to make a difference.

Watch out world, here I come. I will be your next family law attorney, Miss. USA and even the President of the United States. God only knows what my future holds, and thanks to my mom and family, just watch me move mountains.

Chapter 4
MY STORY MATTERS
PARIS NDU

*A strong-minded girl displays confidence.
When you're strong-minded, you're empowered, possess a
healthy self-image, and take responsibility for your life.
The entrepreneurial spirit, by its very nature, requires us
to consider possibilities that most aren't brave enough to.
A girl with a compassionate heart has great influence. Believe
in yourself, never give up on your dreams, be kind and give.
~Paris Ndu*

Six amazing things about me:

Hello! My name is Paris Ndu. I am six years old. I am Miss Cypress 2020 and I want to tell you a story about me because I believe my story matters and I am amazing. I am that six-year-old that was born at 6 months and 2 weeks. Since I was born too early I had to stay in the hospital for a little while and continue to grow and get stronger. Even though things started out for me that way, I am very smart and strong. That makes me so special. I am the only child born to my Nigerian parents. My mom tells me that I was made in India but I was born here in Houston, Texas. My parents promised me 2 siblings, but I am still waiting for them. Don't ask me when, because I don't know when they will come. I am in first grade and I am very kind and loving.

Did I mention that I am a busy little girl? I have a great mom, who will not take excuses and will never take no for an answer. Mama put me on a schedule right from when I was born. That means I have been on schedule all my life. Sunday is my favorite day of the week because I get to be free. I spend time with my family, go to church, eat out at restaurants, and watch my favorite movies. I do taekwondo 3 times a week, music, and dancing 3 times a week. I attend a virtual Barbizon class Monday to Friday evenings and Saturday mornings for modeling and acting. It's hard but I like it. You know why? Because it makes me strong, brave, and confident.

I am blessed, stylish, intelligent, gifted, talented, and creative. When I step out, everyone I pass stares at me. Some will make their way closer and closer to me just to tell me how beautiful I am and how elegant my outfit looks. All these people are total strangers, all of them are saying the same thing. "You look like you could be the future Miss USA, Miss Universe, or Miss World when you grow up." When I was 3 years old, my daycare referred me to the Pageant because of my intelligence and stylish dressing.

My mom waited until I was 5 to take me to the Pageant Houston city interview in August 2020.

I am also a business owner. I am the CEO and Founder of A Fashion Royal and Paris Glows. A Fashion Royal is a clothing company where I sell beautiful clothing and shoes for Princes and Princesses. Paris Glows is an online beauty store, with beauty products and devices for men and women. I have a passion for fashion, style, beauty, and business. I actually get it from my mother. Nigerian people are very stylish and elegant.

My mom is a businesswoman who turns everything into a business. I asked my mom to help me start up my own business. I have a dream that is bigger than the whole world. My main goal in opening my two companies is to contribute to a charity organization that supports children's education in Africa and helps homeless people in America. I do not want anyone to live on the street when I grow up so I want to save them now by helping them go to school. My two companies donate 10% of every sale to a charitable organization that helps children go to school in Africa.

Some really amazing things have happened as a result of me being in a pageant. I used to be a shy little girl. I was raised by my mom, and even though she is very smart she is also very shy and quiet. My mom doesn't want me to grow up like her so she accepted the invitation for me to go to the pageant. Do you know after my first pageant, I got a call back from 3 modeling and acting agencies. I signed with 2 agents. I also got accepted into Barbizon modeling and acting school. This was a dream come true for me because I have wanted to be on TV since I was 3 years old.

I became an Ambassador of the Read to Achieve Program which is a network of readers worldwide. I read stories to children online to ensure that every child who may not have anyone to read to them at home is read to. I also volunteer at a former Daycare Center to read in person. I love the part where I have to go to the daycare center to read. I love the way the little kids always come close to me just to touch my crown, dress or banner. That makes me feel so loved and blessed.

Being in a pageant has taught me a lot of things. Before I went to the pageant I thought pageants were about winning the crown and banner but, no, that is not what it is. I have learned that being in a pageant is also about developing yourself and learning from other people. You will also get the opportunity to meet a lot of other girls your age from all over the country.

Pageants have also taught me tenacity. One day my mom entered my room and said "you've got mail!" I was so excited when we opened the mail. It said that I made it to the Pageant Texas State Finals! I was so excited!! I worked really hard for the pageant but something terrible still happened. There was an acting script that I wanted to try but I didn't see the script until the night before I was supposed to go on stage. So when it was time for the acting competition I heard my name called and I entered the stage. I was very nervous even though I had practiced a lot. You won't believe what happened. Once I got to the stage I realized that I did not understand all of the acting rules. When you hear "slate please," you say your name. When you hear "action," you say your whole line. Then the MC says, "cut". I thought that was the end of my script and I started to leave the stage. The MC had to call me back to the stage because I didn't know that I was supposed to say it one final time.

Imagine you are on stage and you had to go through what I went through. How would you feel? Remember, that was my first time on stage in my life. Because I am a smart little angel, I told myself, "you can do it!" I was as brave and strong as I could be that day. Well, guess what? I continued other activities with a positive mind because I know who I am. I tried to be confident and not let my mistakes bother me.

On the final day, we call it the Finale. I Invited my best friend Adrian to come and see me win. They were calling other Princesses that won trophies, crowns, and banners. Oh no! my name was not being called! I was so nervous and shaking. My heart was beating so fast. I was sitting on my mom's lap. She was consoling me saying, "It's ok baby, you did your best." Even though I did not hear my name called, some of my other friends in the Princess category did win. I was very happy for them and I would give them a high five and say, " good job girl!!"

Then I heard my name! The MC said, "The winner of Our third runner up for Casual Wear Modelling, Paris Ndu!!!" I was so happy. I ran up to the stage to grab my trophy. My friend Adrian and my family were excited for me as well!! Before I could calm down I heard the MC say again, "Our winner for Top Model Search third runner up is Paris Ndu!" I did not just make it to the Texas State Finalist, I also made it to the Nationals! In all, I received 5 trophies in both my first Texas State and first National Pageant which was in Florida. My first time on stage, I surprised everyone, even myself, with my confidence, bravery, determination, excitement, and commitment!!

I love being a pageant queen, but being a Pageant queen is not just about dressing up pretty and wearing a crown. It means so much more. Being a beauty queen is also about serving your community and helping other people. What I like most about being in the pageant is learning new things and making friends from all over the country.

I am changing the world through pageantry. I believe my story matters and it will inspire and motivate the whole world. A Pageant is a place where you can go and develop yourself to be who you want to be in the future. In the pageant, you will meet a lot of caring people. They will help you to be the best you can be. Even if you don't have the experience you can still win, all it takes to be a beauty queen is self-love and self-confidence.

Chapter 5

IT'S A FUN RIDE!

ALEXANDRA WILCOX

"The life you have led doesn't need to be the only life you'll have."
~ Anna Quindlen

Imagine having the same costume and the same song with another girl for back-to-back performances at the talent competition of a national pageant.

Imagine being a mini-me of Miss Universe Iceland 2020 because the two of us share five things in common.

Imagine making friends with girls across the country to do good deeds and make the world a better place.

I am Alexandra Wilcox, the 2021 International Junior Miss Minnesota Jr. Pre-Teen and these are just a few of my experiences so far since I entered the pageant world.

Am I changing the world? I hope so. I think I am. I know for sure that I have definitely changed. I am more confident and have learned a lot along the way. But why enter a pageant in the first place? To be honest, I don't know. My mom saw an open call from National American Miss (NAM) at the beginning of summer 2019. She took me to the training session where we learned that I could win crowns, trophies, and prizes while building life skills along the way. At this training session, I heard "pretty feet" for the first time where I learned to place my feet at the 12 o'clock and 2 o'clock positions for a classic model stance. At the end of this training session, I saw a girl without both arms. She had a beautiful smile on her face. I didn't think much of it at the time, but my mom surely noticed her. After a brief interview with the state directors, my mom and I went home.

A couple of days later, my mom got a text message congratulating me on being chosen as a state finalist. My mom thought it could be a fun thing to do for the summer break in addition to the sports and chess camps I usually attend. She completed the registration and my journey of pageantry began!

It was my very first pageant. I was 6 years old. So, I was in the princess division according to the NAM system. My mom is a researcher. She researched past queens in the princess division and realized that the girls who were winning turned out to be "experienced" even if they were 5 or 6 years old. They may have started pageants as toddlers. Quite a few of them used coaches.

It's a Fun Ride!

With only two months to go before the pageant, my mom decided to seek help from a coach. Coach Faith was very helpful! She quickly taught me everything about the pageants! She also had the best advice on wardrobe. I practiced smiles, walking, reciting my introduction, and interviewing. I love interviews!

Then it was actually time to go to the pageant! I felt nervous and a little anxious because my mom and I didn't know what to expect. My dad was supportive too even though he was not involved in the day-to-day practice. He was my chauffeur and escort. Besides the required competitions, which included formal wear, personal introduction, and interview, I only entered casual wear and photogenic as optional. I tried my best. I made it to the Top 15 among 45 girls. I was so nervous that I almost forgot my introduction. After taking the microphone from the past queen, I said "Hi". Then I forgot my lines! I started looking around, biting my lower lip, and touching the microphone with the other hand. Ten seconds passed. It seemed longer than ever. I got my composure back. I remembered! I was so proud of myself. There were girls who couldn't say a single word before turning around and leaving the stage. It's nerve-racking!

Have I gained life skills? Absolutely yes. The pageant is not all about crowns, trophies, and prizes. It takes courage and confidence in addition to gracefulness to get there. Remember the girl without arms whom I saw at the training session? She got 1st runner-up! She was confident. She danced clogging happily. She did casual wear modeling. She was having fun. Her smiles were contagious!

After the first pageant, I felt obligated to try again because I had so much fun! I loved the opening number dance. I made many friends. Plus I love staying in hotels. My mom was hooked too because she saw potential in me. My interview got the highest score given as a princess, but I could do a lot better with formal wear. Miss Mary became my new coach. She is a dance teacher and works with many young girls. It was through Miss Mary that I found out there was a fourth-grader in my school who competed at NAM as well. She was in the Jr. Pre-Teen division. She did so well that she went on to nationals later that year and got Top 5 in the nation as an All-American Jr. Pre-Teen. It's interesting how I got to know her through pageantry even though we attended the same school!

With the help of Miss Mary, my mom and I became more and more "knowledgeable" of the pageant world. I became more and more confident in walking and continued to hone my speaking skills. Fast forward to 2020, the growth was undeniable.

That year, I originally signed up for Princess of American (POA) to be held in March 2020, but it was canceled due to the pandemic. I got less motivated to practice because the whole world was shut down. I started distance learning and spent most of my time with my family. Luckily, I got a guinea pig as a "pandemic pet" who kept me accompanied and gave me joy. My mom was clever at utilizing the time while I was distance learning. I could see Miss Mary and practice during the school day, of course, wearing masks and applying hand sanitizers from time to time. I remember some of my distance learning classes were done in the car while my mom was driving to or from Miss Mary's. In addition, my mom and I would go for a walk where she asked me to practice modeling on the sidewalk. I remember she helped me practice formal wear at the end of our driveway.

Since the pandemic started, many state pageants were canceled or postponed. Fortunately, the NAM Minnesota/Wisconsin state pageants were relocated to Iowa instead of being canceled. The game was on! The road trip to Iowa was fun. I listened to music, chatted with mom, read books, drew pictures, and even wrote two poems! My mom was extremely helpful to me during this pageant. Due to the pandemic, my dad and my little brother were left home. My mom filled every role that you could think of. She was the driver, the cook, the hair and makeup artist, the wardrobe helper, the cheerleader, and the personal assistant. We packed tons of food—groceries, snacks, and fruits—so that we could eat our own food at the hotel to reduce the potential exposure of Covid-19. We also brought a toaster, a wok, and an electric stove. We both cooked.

My mom could be harsh sometimes. But I personally know that's her shell. On the inside, she is kind, helpful, and funny.

That's my mom! I think she is always very empathic. She knows more about me than anyone else because, well, she is my mom! She can mostly always sense what's happening in my head. She is the one who accompanies me to every single pageant. But she doesn't just help me with my pageants. She is a role model to me, even in other activities.

This was my second pageant although I was no longer a princess contestant. I aged up to be in the Jr. Pre-Teen division. As a 7-year-old, I became one of the youngest in a new age division. In addition to the required competitions, I also signed up for many optionals this time around. I won Best Actress, Best Spokesmodel, and Best Resume. I was the 1st Runner-up to the crown and guess who won? The fourth-grader from my school! When she and I were the last two standing on the stage, I was so nervous. My heart was racing so fast. I could not help turning my head from one judge to another. I think the judges might have noticed my nervousness. On the contrary, she stayed calm and poised. She won! Well-deserved.

I did well at the state. I advanced to the nationals as an All-American Jr. Pre-Teen. Miss Mary warned me that the nationals were a competition among the best. She was not kidding. Not like the state competition, which lasts two days, the nationals last a whole week! There were three stages. And each stage was three times bigger than the one at the state. Can you guess how many contestants were in my division? Eighty-five! There were even more contestants for optional competitions because All-American girls and state queens were competing together. It was really fun to meet talented girls all across the county. That's when I met my "twin". I couldn't have met her without NAM, without pageantry.

Talent was my first competition at the nationals. I dressed in my favorite red Latin dance costume with a red fabric hibiscus on my head. When my mom took me to the backstage waiting area, a girl looked at me with an inviting smile. I immediately noticed her costume. "Are you wearing the same costume as me?" I was in disbelief. My mouth opened. My eyebrows were raised. What a coincidence! We started talking to each other. My nervousness was gone!

As we asked about each other's talents, I found out she had the same music as me, which was *Let's Get Loud* by Jennifer Lopez! I wanted to scream so bad but I knew I should not make loud noises backstage. My mind was definitely screaming! Nobody else knew at this moment. Soon we were in line getting onto the stage. She was directly in front of me. She went first. I wish I could see her performance, but I was behind the screen. "What are the judges going to think?" I was excited and curious. Because we were doing almost the same thing. I felt the motivation to do my best. It seemed I always forgot certain parts of my Cha-cha routine, which happened to me at the state competition, but this time the motivation kicked in and I remembered every single part of my routine. I did better than usual. Everybody including the judges and my mom were confused when they saw me coming up on the stage dressed in the same costume with the exact same music! Déjà vu! Pageantry is not all about crowns and trophies. It builds friendship.

Nationals were super fun with rehearsals, car drawing, and parties. Upon returning from the nationals, my mom and I couldn't stop reading pageant news and competitions worldwide. One day, my mom stumbled on an Instagram announcement: Elísabet Hulda Snorradóttir was crowned as Miss Universe Iceland 2020! As my mom was reading her bio, she got more and more excited. I am half Chinese and a quarter Icelandic. Elísabet Hulda is Icelandic obviously, and she is a student of Chinese Studies! Her Chinese name reads as my nickname. Both of us are ice-skaters. She was crowned on my birthday! My mom could not help leaving a message to her on her Instagram post. She saw it, eventually, and responded. To my surprise, about the same time when the Miss Universe Organization announced the time and location of the postponed 69th Miss Universe Competition, she sent me a video message! In the message, she talked about our shared interests. She also encouraged me to do my best in all my pursuits. She speaks so well! She is as beautiful as she is intelligent. She is as elegant as she is approachable. I loved her even more after we exchanged messages. She is just like me! I wish I could meet her in person, possibly in Hollywood, Florida when she travels to the US for the 69th Miss Universe Competition. I know my mom and even my grandma would love to meet her. My grandma is 100% Icelandic. I am so blessed to find her as my role model. Pageantry builds connections.

Pageantry is not all about the beautiful appearance outside. Pageant girls are changing the world with their platforms and community service projects. A platform is a cause that any pageant girl chooses to volunteer her time to either bring awareness to, raise money, or implement a program she has created that will help address a problem. My platform is ABC, which stands for Allie's Books for Cultures. I am half Chinese and a quarter Icelandic. I have traveled to China, Iceland, and Canada. I also love reading as much as I love traveling. The world would be a better place if people from different cultures understood each other better. So, I hope to bring awareness of cultural diversity through literacy. In addition to my platform, I also volunteer for community service projects. In February, I joined the NAM National Jr. Pre-Teen for her initiative called Compassion Card Drive. Not only did I, but also many Jr. Pre-Teens across the county including International Junior Miss Jr. Pre-teens made cards for senior citizens living in long-term care facilities across the nation. Because of the Covid-19 pandemic, seniors were isolated in their facilities without frequent visits from friends and families. This project was close to my heart because my grandpa was in assisted living due to his Alzheimer's disease before he passed away in October 2020. I made cards for all residents in the memory unit where my grandpa lived and delivered them for Valentine's Day. My grandma was proud of me for doing that. I also had so much fun collaborating with 18 other queens across the county via zoom calls bouncing ideas and planning for the project. In total, we made and delivered 2,027 compassion cards to 48 assisted living and long-term care facilities. We surely made the world a little happier, a little kinder, and a little more loved. A beauty queen is not a queen for herself. Being a queen is a role model of service.

The more I am involved in pageantry, the more I learn about myself, the more tools that I discover to help me grow. I have to tell you about my mindset Coach Amber, whom I got to know after nationals. She taught me to build a healthy self-concept, to be self-confident, and to reframe negative criticism, thoughts, and events to positive ones. Coach Amber made the learning fun and exciting. I learned that you can learn from your mistakes. I also learned vision-boarding. Vision-boarding is when you put things you want to achieve on a board in a collage type. I loved it. It's creative, beneficial for your mindset, and just straight-out fun! Journaling is another tool that I learned to effectively get thoughts out of my mind and onto paper. Coach Amber talked about the fact that writing should not be the only thing you do with journaling. I can also doodle, draw, and sketch. I am grateful to have awesome coaches! They interact with me in a positive, supportive, friendly, and non-critical way. I have been learning a lot!

At the beginning of 2021, NAM and IJM merged into the IAM Pageant Powerhouse. With the merger, there came the

It's a Fun Ride!

opportunities of being appointed queens. I am honored to be named the 2021 International Junior Miss Minnesota Jr. Pre-Teen. The road to the crown doesn't stop there. I am still learning, walking, smiling, dancing, advocating, and most importantly, having fun! It has been a fun ride on the road to the crown. I am having fun with the friends I made through pageantry. I am having fun volunteering in the community and I am preparing for my next pageant competition.

Road to the Crown with Trinity Bush

Chapter 6
UNLEASH YOUR SUPERPOWER
JAKSYN BROWN

*"Be strong and courageous because
you are a superhero...an ordinary kid who chooses
to be extraordinary (or in my case, just extra.)"*
~ *Jaksyn Brown*

I couldn't believe it. I lost...again! My name is Jaksyn Brown. I am a super funny Texan girl who loves having fun and making friends. My favorite funny actor is Kevin Hart. He played in one of my favorite movies, Jumanji. My favorite line from that movie is when he said, "Am I still black?"

I love to kick it with my family every Friday night. One time we kicked it so hard that we stayed up till 3:00 AM celebrating my big sister Jasmine's 24th birthday. We were playing, listening to music, dancing, and stuffing our faces with pizza and my daddy's famous bar-be-que. I also love to eat food....a lot. Every time I eat a big meal I get full but an hour later I am hungry again. My favorite food is candy. It really isn't food, but to me, it is because I eat it all the time. But there's something I love even more than candy. Pageants.

One reason I love doing pageants is that I love to travel. I have traveled to lots of places: California, New York, New Jersey, Louisiana, Florida, Oklahoma, Hawaii ....I'm just kidding. I have not been to Hawaii yet, but my parents have! Another reason I got into pageants is because of my big sister, Bria. She was the person who inspired me to be Miss Texas. I remember when I was 1 year old and I saw her doing a pageant and she won and I was inspired. As I got older I remembered how fun it looked as I watched her on stage. Soon, it was time for me to compete in my first big pageant. So, at the age of 5, I started competing.

Picture it July 2017, Dallas, Texas. I had on a white satin gown and I rocked my signature curly hair. I was so excited! I said my speech perfectly and in my interview, I talked with the judges as best as I could. I tried my best, but when it came down to the final show, I didn't win. I was so sad. Even though it was a tough loss, I loved the pageant so much, I decided to compete again at the national pageant in Anaheim, California. This time I had a different white gown. It had more sparkle to it. When I got on the stage I messed up the walking pattern but I delivered my speech perfectly. My interview outfit was a pink suit with ruffle cuffs.

One of my favorite parts of the pageant was the opening number dance. The song was I'm a Lady by Meghan Trainor and I had so much fun on stage. But guess what. I didn't win....again! So I went back to the Texas state pageant in 2018. This time I was 6 years old and in the first grade. It was the 10th straight day of 100 plus degree weather. (It gets pretty hot in Texas). This time my gown was an aqua blue with millions of rhinestones. It was flowery and it had a small train. It looked very dramatic on stage and I felt so confident in the gown. When I walked out on the stage, my dad said "game time" to help me be confident on stage. It's our good luck tradition. My interview was super amazing! I talked about my favorite foods, my favorite hobbies (swimming), and my favorite book. When all the girls were lined up on stage I was called into the top 10! I felt so happy because I felt like I was really going to win the Texas title. But guess what. I got the first runner up. This time I felt pretty sad, but I didn't cry. Instead, I immediately asked my mom to go swimming. It was so fun because I met a friend at the pool and we ended up being good friends. There was one problem though. I still wanted that crown and banner!

Since I loved competing so much, I decided to take another shot at the national pageant in California. This time, I had a game plan. I practiced my interview twice as hard as before with my mom and other people who helped me, as my coaches, teachers, and family members. I even made a vision board to help me with my next pageant. It had a picture of me with a national crown on because I have always wanted to be a national queen and looking at it every day gave me so much motivation. It had pictures with positive affirmations on it. The affirmations said: I am confident, I am bold, I am talented, I am courageous, I am beautiful. They really helped me stay positive and believe in myself.

Fast forward to Thanksgiving week, 2018. My second trip to the national pageant was nothing short of amazing. At the national pageant, they had so many parties!! PJ parties, neon parties, Disney character dress-up parties, rose gold parties, red, white, and blue parties. The list goes on and on. My favorite party is the Disney-themed party because I get to dress up as Uma. She is my favorite Disney character because she is portrayed by China McClain, a black actress like me. I wore the same aqua blue gown that I did at my Texas state pageant earlier that summer. All of my competitions were flawless. It all came down to the final show. I was so happy to be called into the top 12 and then again in the top 5! I could barely breathe because my heart was beating so fast, but I had to concentrate because the on-stage question was next. My question was: What is special about your state? I talked about the State Fair of Texas and everyone laughed at my answer. Next, it was time to call the runners up and the winner. 4th runner up…..3rd runner up….2nd runner up….. and then there were two. It was down to me and the other final contestant. My heart had never beat so fast. I stood in my aqua blue gown and held my breath. I was thinking, "Please don't call my name!" After what seemed like forever, I felt so amazed when the emcee called out my town as the National Queen! After many tries, my dream of getting that crown and banner finally came true.

This experience taught me that you do not get everything the first time, and from this chapter, you can clearly see I didn't get everything the first time! What I realized is that I had to believe in myself and keep going even though it is hard. I pushed through all the times I didn't win and focused on all the fun I had. I realized that everything is not easy but I sure did learn a lot in the process. When I got a little older, I realized the affirmations I used on my vision board helped me feel better about myself. The truth is, when I was little, I didn't like how I looked and I would always ask my mom to straighten my naturally curly hair. But today, I have learned to embrace what makes me beautiful. I want girls everywhere to feel that they are beautiful just the way God made them.

Pageants have taught me how to talk in front of a large audience and not be shy. Competing in pageants has taught me how to do all of those things and more. For example, it only takes me 2 or 3 days to learn a whole speech. Now, that's a superpower right there. I can also strike up a conversation with just about anyone I meet.

If you feel discouraged do not give up because you can do this! Don't let anyone tell you that you can't. You can do it and you will do it! You are courageous, bold, and talented. You are perfect just the way you are. Be thankful for what you have right now. Don't ever feel bad about yourself because you are amazing. You may think you are just an ordinary kid but you are actually extraordinary. Remember you are a superhero in your own way. So unleash your superpowers! You may not have reached your big goal yet, but if you stay positive and believe in yourself, you can achieve anything you put your mind to. Now, go out there and try it again, again, and again. You will be surprised at what you can accomplish with a little bit of sparkle, a whole bunch of funny, and a positive attitude.

Chapter 7
THE TWINS WHO CHASE THEIR DREAMS
CAYLEE AND ABIGAIL

No one can make you feel inferior without your consent."
~ Eleanor Roosevelt (Caylee)

"If you hear a voice within you say 'you cannot paint,'
then by all means paint, and that voice will be silenced."
~ Vincent Van Gogh (Abigail)

We may be twins, but we are one of a kind. We are Caylee and Abigail Hauck. We are twins who may look alike, but we are individually unique. We were not looking for pageants, but the pageant life came for us.

One day 2 years ago our mom received a card in the mail inviting us to come to an open session for the National American Miss. We were so excited. Our parents had researched the pageant and discovered that one of the rules included no make-up allowed for our age group. We both attended the open call with our mom and learned about the pageant which was to be held in March 2019. During that open call, we were interviewed but had to wait to hear if we got accepted. After waiting for what felt like forever, we both got in and started preparing for our first pageant at the age of 6. We were competing in the 2019 North Carolina Princess category.

Our mom helped us pick out our gowns and we worked on our speeches. We competed with many girls and made so many friends. We also competed in the Top Model, Photogenic, and Casual Wear Modeling optional competitions. We learned a lot from the whole experience. We learned above all that we were there to support one another as twin sisters no matter who won what prize.

That first year, Caylee got 2nd runner-up Top Model, Art Contest winner, and first runner-up in the National American Miss North Carolina Princess. That was a huge success to us for not knowing about pageants and starting only about 3 months earlier. Abigail did not place however she received some awards one of which was the fan award.

Caylee got invited to Nationals the very first year and since Abigail did not, Caylee gave her sister a couple of her roses, and then she gave her queen's roses to three other girls who did not win and were upset. Caylee made their day so much brighter.

We leveled up to the Junior Preteen category the following year for the state. We practiced and prepared so much then the COVID-19 hit so the pageant was canceled. We decided to still go for the appointed state title and we both got in. We were both 3rd and 4th runner up for the National American Miss Junior Preteen. Caylee became the 2020 Miss Mecklenburg County Junior Preteen and Abigail became the 2020 Miss Charlotte Junior Preteen. We were excited about the chance to go to Nationals again. The appointed state queen was not the same as being in person but we were able to wear our gowns and do everything from home though we missed our new friends.

During Nationals we were more nervous than before, but we had a great time and enjoyed supporting the other girls. We did not place at all during Nationals, but we learned how it works and knows that we can do it again if we are blessed to qualify again. Our family was so proud of us. We had our mom, dad, big brothers Alex and Thomas with us. Even our grandmother, who we call mommom, came along.

We learned teamwork, confidence, and overcame stage fright. We learned to never give up and if you do not succeed the first time, try it again! There were a lot of hugs and a lot of tears both happy, and scared. At the end of Nationals, we asked our mom and dad if we could give our roses up to the friends and girls who put themselves aside to help us and gave us great advice. The main thing is everyone wants you to succeed but you never give up no matter how hard you might think it is. We left the pageant with a great sense of determination.

During the off-time, we have become Read to Achieve Ambassadors and competed in the virtual Miss Diamond Universe. Abigail won the competition and is the 2021 Miss Diamond Universe Princess. Caylee won the Miss Diamond Universe Photogenic award. We were so excited! It's the steps you take to keep going no matter what gets thrown your way that really builds character. We also love volunteering, sending greeting cards to Senior Homes, donating to our Goodwill, and trying to build a store online for our handmade items.

We love to share with others, to show them that anything is possible and that everyone is unique. That is why the crown is so important. It is a reminder to never give up on your dreams no matter where the road leads.

Although we are twins, we are still unique. We love the chances we get to have our voices heard and talents showcased. We hope to try more pageants in the future, but until then we will continue to cheer on our friends at the National American Miss pageant, dance in our spare time, and volunteer.

The Twins who chase their dreams

As twin sisters, competing in the same pageant has been exciting and can also be a lot of work. We are currently practicing for the 2021 National American Miss North Carolina Junior Preteen which is scheduled for July 2021. We are nervous, however, we will do our best and try hard. If you see us please say hello as we are the twins who do everything together but love to live uniquely on our own. That's what being twins is really all about. We root for each other. We are our own best friends and cheerleading section. We can laugh, cry, and get scared but when we look to the side we are right there for one another.

Road to the Crown with Trinity Bush

Chapter 8
A NATURAL CROWN
JAZEL BELLA JOHNSON

*"Always be confident in all you think &
do because it determines the success of your outcome...
Be Great, Be You, Be Blessed"*
~Jazel Bella Johnson

"Confidence is Key." I was always taught to love who I am on the inside and outside. I've always had this different power about me. There was nothing I felt like I couldn't achieve if I prayed and put my mind to it. Every evening I would say my prayers before going to bed and each morning, I would say, "I am smart, I am kind, I am beautiful, I love God and I love me." This is what has given me the confidence to achieve great things, whether performing a monologue, dancing across the stage, or designing "Everything Fashion." I know that God loves me and I wear a special Natural Crown each day I wake up. Being able to be who you are and know whose you are, is the key to my self-confidence.

My first pageant was really scary for me because I had never done anything like that before. Everyone looked so prepared and ready to get the crown. I thought I would do well, but how do you completely prepare for a pageant when it is something completely new? At that moment, I had to remember, "I already wear a crown!" So, I did my best and got an invitation to Nationals, which gave me an opportunity to go to Hollywood, California.

Preparing for Nationals took another level of preparation. When the date for Nationals arrived, everything was ready, my dress, shoes, outfits, earrings, and all my pageant goodies. It took us five hours to arrive at our destination. When we arrived I excitedly anticipated making new friends. At rehearsals, I met and became friends with two new besties and tons of other pageant sisters. We would always wish each other luck when doing a performance and our friendship strengthened as we hung out and rode rides with each other at Disneyland.

Next, I had to do rehearsals with my dad for formal wear. We both looked really good doing it. We would practice wherever we went. The hallways, the hotel room, and even going into the stores. Practice makes perfect. My favorite competition was the interview. If you ever have a hard time interviewing, just be natural and try not to add on or ramble because then you are gonna start to forget the words and not be authentically you.

A Natural Crown

It was finally time for the finals. I put on my pink dress and my glitter heels. When my Dad and I lined up I had to do my confidence check, I remembered, " I already wear a crown" and I was ready to hit the stage. I was #45 representing Philadelphia, Pennsylvania. My dad and I met different girls and their fathers. It was a moment I will always remember. It was our turn to go on the stage. I was really nervous and excited at the same time. We did our walk and went off the stage. It was amazing, I felt as if I had just walked on the Fashion Week stage. After that, we had to do an independent walk. Then we started to line up for the award ceremony.

The pageants allowed me to look at things differently and changed the way I do everything. Another great thing I gained from pageants was my love for community service. This was something my family has always done with me. So I was able to combine my love for serving my community along with my pageant participation. So after winning a number of titles at nationals, I was again filled with joy and excitement with my pageant experience.

Another opportunity presented itself and this is by far one of my fondest memories to date. I was asked to appear on the nationally syndicated Fox 29, The Q Show for an interview as "Miss Philadelphia." to speak about everything pageantry and myself. This is just one example of how pageantry will open up new doors and opportunities. When we received this call I was so happy and excited. A week later it was my time to shine. I got all dolled up and dressed in my favorite royal blue gown. As I walked into the television station I felt a little nervous and anxious, so I recited my mantra, "I already wear a crown." I met Mr. Q, he asked me questions and I even taught him to do the catwalk. The experience was life-changing. This was a moment where I felt like I could give hope to other young girls who may have issues with self-confidence, stage fright, or using their voice. I wanted to use this experience to encourage them to believe they can do and be anything they want to be with preparation, prayer, and persistence.

A few months later it was time for the next pageant week. I had never felt so ready to do something. I walked into the competition ready to go. I had done my rehearsals, the categories, and personal introduction. The award ceremony was starting. My heart was beating so fast. I was really scared and nervous at the same time, then I remembered, "I already wear a crown." Still to this day, I will never forget them calling my name for 8 titles, I was overjoyed and beyond grateful. They literally called my name eight times. I won Miss Pennsylvania Jr. Pre-Teen Talent, Miss Pensylvania Jr. Pre- Teen Actress, Miss Pennsylvania Jr. Pre-Teen Casual Wear Modeling, Miss Pennsylvania Jr. Pre-Teen Most Promising Model, and Miss Pennsylvania Jr. Pre-Teen 2nd Runner Up, Miss Pennsylvania Jr. Pre-teen Photogenic 1 st Runner Up, Miss Pennsylvania Top Model Search 3rd Runner Up, and a number of other awards. It was unbelievable. I did it.

A Natural Crown

I received another invitation to Nationals and I decided to change everything I did. I got new colors for all my outfits, shoes, and even my talent from tap to jazz. I practiced every day until I thought it was great. Always remembering, practice makes perfect. Nationals were almost here and I could not wait.

My first day was just like the previous year. I checked in and caught up with my awesome pageant sisters. The next day I had rehearsals and I could not wait to see my pageant besties. Pageants are not just about winning and getting crowns and sashes. It's about gaining your confidence and meeting new people. During Nationals there was an award given out called Miss Personality. When they called my name I was surprised and proud. One thing I learned about pageants is that crowns come in all shapes and sizes, but your Natural Crown comes from your Heart and from God. A Natural Crown is not a physical crown it is something that has been inside of you and ready to come out. "Natural Beauty is the Best Beauty". Be You, Be Confident, and always wear your Natural Crown!!

Road to the Crown with Trinity Bush

Chapter 9
FROM NONVERBAL TO SPEAKING ON A NATIONAL STAGE!
ABIGAIL HAUSER

"Thou she be little, she is fierce"
~ Shakespeare.

When I was a year old, I wouldn't talk to anyone or make any sounds besides crying, this made communicating with my family very difficult. My nonverbal condition was so extreme that I started speech therapy at only 18 months old. Due to my extreme speech condition, even the speech therapists were challenged to get me talking, which is why my 1st language isn't English, it's American Sign Language. Fortunately, I picked up ASL easily so my mom was challenged to learn my new way of communicating.

When I did begin to talk, I would only talk to my mom and sister, though occasionally my dad. I was scared & nervous, not really wanting to talk to anyone because I talked differently. It took me two whole years to talk to one of my regular caregivers and 6 months to initiate a conversation with my preschool teacher whom I saw every day.

I was four years old and entering Kindergarten when we moved to Iowa. A short while later I got a letter in the mail inviting me to attend a pageant open call, asking me if I wanted to learn more about their pageant being held that spring. I attended the Open Call with my mom and knew right away that I wanted to take part in this amazing pageant, I mean, what little girl doesn't want to be a princess with a sparkly crown. My mom, knowing that I could get many benefits from this, agreed that it could help me with my fear of talking with others!

During pageant weekend, I made many friends and had a lot of fun! The most important thing though was that I actually talked. They were kind and didn't laugh or question when I talked differently, the other girls just accepted me and my differences. I didn't feel out of place when I talked to the other girls nor did I feel strange when I talked to the judges in our one-on-one interviews. I had finally begun to come out of my shell of quietness and really started speaking to others. The first year I didn't place in anything or get to go to nationals, but I had the time of my life! My mom saw the increase in my confidence that weekend and has been one of my biggest pageant supporters since. She no longer questions the value of natural pageants.

From nonverbal to speaking on a national stage!

My mom said if I wanted to continue with pageants, I had to talk to businesses around me about sponsorship fees and to help with my communication skills as well. Even if I didn't get a sponsor check, it gave me interview practice and made me more comfortable at the pageant talking to others. Little did we know that the next year, I would be confidently talking on a national stage, in front of hundreds!

One time, in my second year in the princess division, I completely forgot my introduction. But I held it together, thought about it, and soon remembered my lines, and kept going. I was a little nervous but I didn't cry, I just kept thinking until I remembered. Unfortunately, the time was up and I was only halfway through my introduction, so I knew I most likely wouldn't win, but I did my best and that's what truly mattered. My mom said she could see in my eyes that the wheels were turning as I worked to remember my introduction and that my poise and confidence after forgetting was a win for the weekend. I definitely learned a lesson as I have never again forgotten my introduction.

Another example of the way pageants build confidence happened a few years ago. I was competing in formalwear on the National Stage when I stepped on the edge of my dress and stumbled. Without missing a beat of showing even the slightest bit of panic, I just kept going. I learned from pageantry to keep going and persevere because you never know, the judges may be looking for a girl who keeps going even when she makes a mistake. I was confident even in the other portions of the competition after that because it's who I am. Once again, my mom LOVED the fact that I had such a graceful reaction to this formalwear stumble because it showed her my character. That I could be confident regardless of mistakes. To her, it was a win for Nationals even if I didn't place or win the overall competition. She loved my reaction so much that she kept sharing the video of my stumble and reaction with others.

The many life skills I have gained from all my pageant experiences have pushed me in areas outside of pageants as well, from talking to businesses about my service work to talking to adults about my future goals. The friends I have made throughout the pageants are all so inspiring! I love how you can find things in common with girls who you would never have met if you hadn't done pageants. Even my mom has made new lifelong friends!

Another benefit I got from joining pageants, besides making many lifelong friends and learning life skills is a greater love for community service. Because I have so much fun and joy helping others, I founded my own movement, called *Rockin' It with Kindness*, to encourage kids to make a difference in their communities, even if they are younger than everyone else. Pageants helped me with creating connections that helped me grow and expand my movement.

From nonverbal to speaking on a national stage!

I know that I am different from everyone else, yet I still refuse to let it hold me back. I continued to move forward in my journey towards winning a national pageant. In July 2019 I decided to compete in another pageant. I got 1st runner up at state! I was disappointed but happy since my friend won! Being 1st runner up allowed me to compete at nationals where I was competing against other girls who had competed with this pageant before. I was a little nervous, as always, but I had lots of fun. Guess what? I won! I was so excited! A girl, still actively involved with speech therapy, had just won a mainstream national pageant! By the time I went to bed late that night, I was exhausted, but I still dreamed of the opportunities that being a national title holder with speech differences would offer to so many others just like me.

I know that I am not your average pageant girl and I LOVE that! But the thing is, you CAN'T be an average pageant girl, because people aren't the same. Everyone has their own backstory. When you think of a pageant girl, you probably just think of a girl wearing a fancy dress with lots of makeup and talking about her lovely lifestyle. But, we pageant girls aren't that, and we should be proud of who we are.

I really want people to know that pageants aren't just about who's the prettiest, richest, or who's perfect. It's about who you are on the inside and anyone can do a pageant, learn life skills, or even win! No matter what your life situation is!

YOU ARE WHO YOU ARE AND YOU ARE AWESOME!

Pageantry has made me much more confident (and talkative) in every aspect of my life; from school to Taekwondo (where I'm working on my 2nd degree Black Belt) to Girl Scouts to leading *Rockin' It with Kindness* and so much more!

If I can go from being nonverbal and learning American Sign Language in speech therapy, to talking on a national stage in front of hundreds, anyone can do a pageant, no matter their age, disabilities, or life situations, even YOU!

Chapter 10
IT'S SO MUCH BIGGER THAN A CROWN
REAGHAN DANEE

"I'm living my best life"
~Reaghan Danee

I'm so thankful, I found pageants because I'm good at them. The best advice my mother gave me is "don't look down when you are walking, don't cry if you don't win, hold your head up high, and be happy for the winner. Never give up!!!! Be strong, you rock, keep trying, be courageous. God created us to do our best and we are all precious in his eyesight." My mom's favorite pageant motto is "do your best and have fun". My first pageant, I entered was the year after my mother received a flyer in the mail in June 2019. I did not know anything about pageants. I had never watched or seen a pageant before. I was extremely nervous and scared to compete. The funny thing is my mom seemed to have a lot of confidence in me. She told me I could win and I believed her.

Not only did my mom enter me into the pageant, she asked me if I wanted to compete in actress, casual wear, and top model. I told her yes. My mom asked one of our family friends to help me find clothing. I was so excited about going shopping and getting new clothes. Ms. Leah asked me what type of formal dress I wanted. I told her I wanted something fashion-forward and very fashionable. I want to look different than the other girls, so the judges would remember me. I ended up getting a royal blue romper with pretty sequins on the top and with an overskirt. In hindsight my choice was not the best one nor was it formal wear.

The day came for the pageant. I was extremely overwhelmed with emotions. I didn't want to let my mom down because she paid a lot of money for me to compete. During the registration process, I met a lot of girls. The girls were so nice and were very encouraging. The pageant occurred over a three-day period. My first optional competition was actress. I learned my script the day before. While I was performing I forgot my script. I was proud of myself because I did not cry or run off the stage. I finished the rest of the competition without any problems. I was so excited for the finale night. I had a lot of friends and family there to support me. Out of 115 beautiful girls in my division, I won Miss Personality, Miss Spirit, Top Fan Club, and 2nd runner up in the top model. There were a lot of girls crying and mad. I was so happy I won several trophies. That was my first time ever winning trophies. After the finale show, I told my mother I was happy about the trophies and I was ok that I did not make it to nationals. I realized I received the opportunity to go to nationals in California after I talked to my mom.

As I prepared for my first National pageant my mother hired a pageant coach. I worked with them weekly on my interview skills, walking, and stage presence. My coach encouraged me to find a platform I was passionate about. I chose Susan G. Komen Foundation in honor of my Nana. My Nana passed away from breast cancer when I was 4 years old. My mom and I were still struggling with her death. We both decided to volunteer to give back to others and to help us both in the healing process. My Nana's favorite color was yellow. Everything I wore during competition week was yellow. When I wear yellow I feel that my Nana is on the stage with me and that makes me very happy.

During my first national competition, I learned a lot of things and met a lot of new people from around the United States. Currently, I still talk to some of the girls I met. I told my mom after the national finale I want to come back to compete and win the state of Texas. I was very determined to meet my goal. I worked hard with my pageant coach. A month later I received my pageant scores. I scored 47 of 100 girls. My coach told me to find local pageants to compete so I could practice my skills. I competed in 2 local pageant competitions and won the state title. In July

2020, I competed in the North Texas appointed state title. The North Texas pageant was virtual due to COVID 19. I had to submit a 30-second video recording of my personal introduction, resume, pageant headshot picture, and a 300-word essay. Also, I had a thirty-minute zoom interview. My mom was surprised the interview was 30 minutes long. The next night my mom received an email stating I won the junior preteen division. My mom was so excited. I read the email and started screaming!!!!! I was so happy!!! My mom told me my hard work had paid off.

In August 2020, I went to Houston, Texas to get crowned. That was one of the best weekends of my life. While I was in Houston one of the pageant officials told me that I scored the highest in the interview process throughout the state of Texas. My interview score beat adults. Not only did I have the highest score, I had the hardest judge. The reason why my interview was so long is that the judge enjoyed talking to me. I have gained five sister queens. Sister queens are girls from different age groups who are crowned at the pageant. We try to get together after the pageant as much as possible to hang out. My sister queens encourage me to do my best.

During the week of Thanksgiving, I attended my second national pageant as a state queen. I was so happy to see some of my old friends and make new friends. I competed in several of the optional competitions such as actress, fresh faces, casual wear, runway, and spokesmodel. My favorite optional is spokesmodel.

The best moment of the pageant is when I made it to the top 12 and won the people's choice award. I could not believe so many people voted for me. When the announcer called my name I was in shock.

Friendships are the best side of pageantry. Pageants are more than winning a crown; it is about the life lessons you learn. You only win the crown and title for one year. What you do during your reign is what truly matters such as being a positive role model, having a positive attitude, treating people well, and being courageous.

Road to the Crown with Trinity Bush

Chapter 11
MY FIRST BIG WIN
CORTNEY LISBY

"Why fit in when you were born to stand out."
~Dr. Suess

Your 2017 Miss South Carolina Princess is Cortney Lisby! I was in shock when I heard my name. It seemed like I was frozen before I went to accept my sash and crown. I looked into the audience and saw my mom hollering and I knew this was real. This was the start of my new pageant journey.

Before I go any further let me take you back to when it all started. My mom entered me into my very first pageant, a glitz and glam type pageant when I was six months old. I competed in this pageant until I was four years old. During my time with the pageant, I brought home many awards and trophies, but never the title. While competing in the pageant I earned a scholarship to a Modeling Agency, I also received a letter in the mail inviting me to come to compete in the Miss South Carolina pageant. I wanted to break my shyness and build my self-confidence, so my mom did her research on the pageant system and we decided to give it a go. This is when my real pageant journey began.

On June 23, 2016, I competed in my first natural pageant, I was only 5 years old. I went into this pageant weekend attached to my mom's hip. As I went to each rehearsal, I got up on stage to practice and when I was done, I hurried back to find my mom. During pageant weekend I experienced a lot of things I had never experienced in my previous pageant. With this pageant I had to get on stage and say my personal introduction, I went into a room and conducted a two-minute one-on-one interview with six judges, and I was able to have an escort for formalwear.

After competing all weekend, the last day finally came. This was the crowning day. For my very first natural pageant, I received state finalist, 1st runner-up casual wear, and overall 2nd place in the Queen's court. Although I did not win the title I was headed to Nationals in Anaheim, California.

Heading to Nationals was another first. This was my first trip on an airplane and I was headed to Anaheim, CA for nine days over Thanksgiving weekend. Nationals were amazing, there were girls from all over. The competition at Nationals was very tough. I was still a little shy, but my mom told me to go out on the stage and do my best. Although I did not place, I enjoyed the experience

My First Big Win

and knowledge I gained and was looking forward to going back to Nationals again.

After competing in my first year of the natural pageant my mom asked me, how did I like the pageant? I told her I enjoyed it and was looking forward to competing in this pageant again.

Well, here we are again a year later and I'm getting ready to compete for my second year with the natural pageant. I went into pageant weekend so full of confidence that I had a feeling this was my year. When I went through check-in, I spoke to everyone with boldness. At rehearsals I no longer wanted to sit by mom, I wanted to be where all the other girls were. I went to rehearsals, placed my belongings by mom, and off I went to make some new friends.

We always have a pajama party on the first night and on that night, I got up on that stage and danced like nobody was watching, but little did I know I was being watched by the choreographers. I was one of the girls chosen to compete in a little dance-off, each girl had two minutes to dance. It was finally my turn to dance, everyone looked at the Dj booth and said, "hit it Dj" and he started to play "Watch Me Whip" and I danced and danced and danced my whole 2 minutes. Once all the girls had a chance to dance the crowd got to help decide on a winner by screaming and clapping the loudest for their favorite contestant. Well, here it is down to me and another girl and I hear the choreographer say the 2017 Miss

Dance Contest winner is Cortney Lisby. I was so excited; this was the start of a great weekend.

It was Saturday I'm up early to get ready for my optional, and the first was casual wear. I go over my routine one more time before we leave the room. Once in the ballroom, my mom walks me to my seat and she says, "Get on stage, give it your best, make eye contact with the judges, smile big, and have fun!" When it was my turn to take the stage, I went out there and gave it my all. As the day went on, I got on that stage time after time, and I gave my all every time.

Finally, it was time for my favorite part of pageant weekend, formal wear. I love putting on my formal gown and my sparkly shoes. I also get to be escorted by my granddaddy. We have the best time sitting together, talking and laughing until it's our time to take the stage. It's lights, camera action when I take the stage. I feel beautiful like a polished diamond. That weekend I had so much confidence I felt I rocked my formal wear.

Sunday is the crowning day. The only thing left to do is my interview and the final rehearsals before the finale'. The time is near and I'm getting dressed in my production number outfit. The finale' a performance in which we all wear a special outfit and perform a special dance together. My mom takes me to the dressing room to get settled, she drops me off with the other girls and heads into the ballroom to get ready to watch the final show.

My First Big Win

As I'm waiting with the other girls, we go over the dance again and we play games until it is showtime. When it's showtime I take the stage along with the other girls and I dance my heart out. Once the dance is over my mom meets me in the dressing room to get dressed in my formal gown for the crowning.

Here it is the moment we have all been waiting for; the results. That night, I won 1st runner-up casual wear, and "your new 2017 Miss South Carolina Princess is.....Cortney Lisby." I won! I really won! I now have the opportunity to represent the great state of South Carolina, the home of smiling faces and beautiful places. Not only did I win the title, but I gained five bonus sisters that I built a lifelong bond with.

As we are heading home, I'm still full of excitement over my win. Being crowned a queen has some rewards such as traveling to different states to make appearances, meeting new people young and old, being in parades, and getting dolled up to speak at certain events. There are also a few downs to being a queen when you're a little six-year-old girl, such as having to be awakened from naps to practice or not being able to play with your friends due to an event. It's okay because I learn to manage it all with my mom's help. I was able to balance my personal life and pageant life by following a schedule that my mom made for me and made sure I stuck to it.

Pageants are something I do not see giving up any time soon. Being able to do pageants is a passion that I long for. I love being on the big stage and competing. I enjoy the opportunity to travel, meet new friends and compete in different optionals. Being a beauty queen is not always about the glitz and glam, but it allows you to show your beauty from the inside out. One may ask if doing pageants is easy, in my opinion, it is easy, but you must be willing to put in the work. You must have courage, patience, confidence, and patience.

So today you are no longer looking at a shy little five-year-old girl attached to her mom's hip. You are looking at a small but mighty, strong-willed 10-year-old who is full of confidence and is sure to light up a room when she enters, not only has this pageant system allowed me to gain self-confidence, but this pageant system has taught me how to conduct an interview, how to speak in public, how to be ambitious and how to live out my dreams.

For those of you who are thinking about competing in a pageant, I say go for it. I'll leave you with a quote my mom tells me at the beginning of every pageant. "Why fit in, when you were born to Stand out." Signing off from the great state of South Carolina, I am Cortney Lisby.

Chapter 12
THE POWER OF...
LACI ELLA BROWN

"Always stay true to yourself and never allow insecurity to diminish the light that shines brightly within you."
~ Laci Ella Brown

When I was born, I was a preemie and weighed 3lbs 14oz. I spent almost two months in the NICU. My mom told me that the first time she came to see me, the doctors and nurses in the NICU told her that I was very feisty. My mom said, "What has she done in two days that makes you call her feisty?" The doctor said that I kept pulling the tube out of my nose. I guess I didn't want it there – even as a 3lb preemie, I knew what I wanted. My family gets a good laugh from that story because I have been "Miss Feisty" ever since.

I've always been a very confident, outgoing person and I've never been intimidated by anyone or anything. I began participating in pageants at the age of seven years old and I won the very first pageant I ever competed in. Winning the title of the 2016 Miss Missouri Jr Preteen in one of the top natural pageant systems was a wonderful experience and it gave my confidence level a little boost. However, when I turned ten years old and I became a preteen, my confidence level went down a little bit. It wasn't because of anything that happened to me, I was just becoming a preteen and my view or perspective of things seemed to be very different from what it had been in the past. I began to feel self-conscious about things and I began to doubt myself. I don't think this is unique to me. I think that most preteens go through this, but it was new to me and I honestly didn't even know what was going on.

When I first began competing in pageants, I always felt comfortable and confident. However, the first year that I went to a national pageant and competed as a preteen, it was a very different experience. I was 10 years old and I was the youngest girl competing in the preteen age group. I was so nervous and self-conscious. During the pageant, I was so stressed that I eventually gave up and "decided" that I wasn't going to do my best because I was like "What's the point - I'm not going to win anyway."

My mom and I are very, very, very close and I love her more than anything in the whole wide world, but sometimes we clash because I am a very opinionated person and my mom likes things to be done the way she wants. (And she has the right to…I mean she IS the mom). During the national pageant that year, we clashed a lot. Because it was my first year as a preteen, I wanted to be more independent, but I was also dealing with a lot of feelings of insecurity that I had never dealt with before and I didn't know how to express that to my mom.

I was also trying to be older, especially during my on-stage competitions, and I wasn't being myself. My mom said to me "I could tell when you were doing your personal intro, that you were trying to be older and it wasn't natural." All of these things - my insecurity, my mom and I fighting, me giving up – probably added more stress and contributed to my negative mindset.

That year at the national pageant, I didn't place in the Top 10 and I was so disappointed. Looking back, I realize that I made a mistake. I should not have given up and I should have given my best to the competition. I was very prepared for the competition, but I gave up and I should never have done that. Even though I was disappointed that I didn't place, I wasn't upset with myself. I know now that I didn't realize what was going on with me and I look at it as a learning experience. I also know that I should have talked to my mom to help me get through the doubt and insecurity that I was dealing with.

In 2020, I made the decision that I wanted to return to the national pageant and compete in the preteen category again. I knew I wanted to try and make up for my previous pageant experience and I felt like I needed to redeem myself because I believed that I was a much better competitor than I displayed the previous year. However, the world was impacted by a worldwide pandemic and the pageant experience was very different from what it had been in the past. Everything was virtual.

I competed in my first virtual pageant and I won the title of Preteen Miss Great Plains. I was going back to the national pageant! I was so excited, but I knew I had a lot of work to do. I participated in several virtual pageants to improve myself and to get feedback from judges that would help me identify areas to work on. I worked for six months with several different coaches to perfect my interview skills, my on-stage skills, my public speaking skills, and my platform.

I became very creative with my community service activities because the pandemic prevented me from doing in-person activities. I created my platform Laci's Hunger Games as a challenge to bring awareness to and help end food insecurity in children. I created a logo and I completed over fifteen community service projects/activities in the midst of the pandemic - including raising over $580 for a local food distribution network that provides healthy foods and snacks for children who don't have food on the weekend or during times when school is not in session.

The Power of...

When it was time for the national pageant, I felt fully prepared to compete for the two national titles of Preteen Miss and Junior Ambassador.

It was a very different experience from the previous national pageant. I wasn't nervous at all. I was myself and I believed I could win. I was so at ease on stage and there was this indescribable feeling of accomplishment and confidence even before the final show. I felt like any mistake I might make could not knock me down.

During the optional competition awards show, I won all of the competitions that I competed in except for one, and I placed second runner up in that competition. I was very excited to be crowned the overall National Spokesmodel winner in the junior division for my speech on food insecurity in children. I was crowned the overall National Casual Wear Modeling winner in the junior division. I felt like I had accomplished and improved so much in the last year and I was so proud of all of my hard work.

At the final show, I was so confident and so ready to hear the results of the national winners. My name was called for Top 10 and then Top 5 for both of the titles that I truly wanted to win. I was so excited! Unfortunately, I was not the winner for either title, but I did place 2nd runner up for both the Preteen Miss and the Junior Ambassador national titles.

Although, I was very disappointed that I didn't win, I was most grateful. I had placed second runner up for both titles and I knew that my hard work had paid off because I believed in myself and I competed and I did my absolute best.

Comparing my performance in both national pageants, I could definitely see a change in my level of confidence, and I believe that one of the biggest obstacles that I overcame was my poor attitude and mindset.

I never understood the saying "If you think it, you can be it". However, now that I've been in a situation that this applies to, I completely understand what it means.

What I want pageant girls, or any girl, to know is that it really is about your mindset and the power of positive thinking. Before I had this experience, I brushed off and dismissed that what I think to myself is very powerful and I didn't always take it into consideration with everything that I did. Now I do because I know what the mind can do - it literally controls your actions.

When you think something and you continue to think it, even though you're not purposefully trying to show it or behave in that way, you can make it happen and not be conscious about it. Your thoughts are powerful and even your words have power. When you say something, you can speak it into your reality. So, keep your words and your mindset positive on all things – big and small. If

The Power of...

your mindset is positive and you believe you can, you will accomplish big things.

I came into the world as a 3lb 14oz preemie, but my personality has always been big. With my new outlook of maintaining a positive mindset in all things, I know that I have the power to achieve any goal I set for myself. I cannot wait to show the world all of the amazing things Miss Feisty will accomplish.

Road to the Crown with Trinity Bush

Chapter 13
THE DIRECT AND CHANGING PATH
CLORIESA DARDEN

"Nevertheless I will persist because history is always watching"
~ *Cloriesa*

I was not expecting this. I had a plan, and I was determined to follow it. I have always been afraid of failing and falling off the tracks of my plan. However, I am still the hardest working procrastinator you will ever meet. I have always known what I want. I want to be a human rights attorney. I want to attend Howard or Hampton University, but realistically it will be Winston-Salem University. See, that is what I had to learn on my own. Being realistic. Of course, my teachers and mom have always taught me this, but it always felt as if it was in a belittling manner. Over time I have come to realize for myself that reality opens doors for failure, but failure opens doors for opportunities.

Imagine a little girl watching an older girl reach for her dreams. I was once that little girl and I am living up to be that older girl. So, who am I now?

I used to be a principals' list and honor roll student who loved school. In Math, I was told about a school that could lead me on a quicker path to my dreams. That is what we want right? A path that can guarantee success and a secure wallet. So, I studied and took the test to get into school. I authored my essay about how I loved challenges and how I would overcome any hardships that came my way. Was I lying? Not exactly. But, I understand that it is easier to say what they want to hear.

Say what they want to hear? Knowing me, it is easier said than done. I am the type who likes to speak my opinions. So, when my mother first mentioned a pageant to me, I instantly said no. Pageants were not my cup of tea. In my head it was all about money and beauty; pretending to care about others when you just want a crown and prize.

I gave in though.

In the first few months of 2019, the words "time" and "management" slapped me in the face. I had so many things to do and I wasn't managing my time well.

That same year I learned that my biological father had passed away. I didn't know what to do or feel *"How can I grieve for a man I had never met?"*

That was a dilemma that had led to calls and calls from strangers I didn't even know existed. I have two older brothers and one younger brother. Not only am I not the youngest but I am also the only girl on my biological dad's side.

The next month was filled with studying, tests, writing, pageant practices, and memorizing a speech. And a new family member that I was stuck with. Time was crunching down, and nothing stressed me out more than my mother asking me "Have you...?" "Did you...?" "Cloriesa!".

At least I was accepted into Early College. I barely made it, but it was good enough for me.

Pageant time!

I spoke to one of my brothers and he said he was coming to my pageant.

The anticipation, the counting down. I was competing against older girls; I was not even in their age category! *Who will be Queen?*

It was me!

It felt so weird and good at the same time. I was not crying; I was in the middle of the stage with the lights blinding me. Though seeing my older brother sitting there felt nice. Even though he and my family were the loudest people in the building.

So, maybe pageants were my thing. And they were not filled with snobby girls. I got a little taste of black girl magic in that pageant. I even won Miss Congeniality!

This was when everything for me truly started to change. I recognized a new passion of mine. I got to speak and give light on the behalf of the African Americans who do not have the opportunity to do so. The pageant was mainly black, so when my pageant coach suggested that I continue to the State competition in Winston Salem, I was not up for it, but I said sure anyway. I had been getting more comfortable saying yes.

Another stressful month filled with anticipation. I was worried about the money. My mother always told me I would not have to worry about money, but I still did. My parents had the favor of God. They always told me I had a light that would shine bright. Sometimes it felt like that light did not exist. I honestly had no idea what they were talking about most of the time. My coach even told me I had the winning smile. I did not know what she was talking about either. Maybe that is what is holding me back, sometimes; the worrying about the future or my small insecurities.

It was weird participating in the state competition. There were not many other girls of color. I made some friends. Good friendships that will last for a while and some just for the moment. There I was! On stage standing with the other runners-up. I placed third runner-up. I was surprised. Not that bad for my second pageant and my first national organization pageant. I placed in some other categories, but not Spokes Model. I like being a Spokesmodel.

In most of the pageants, many girls did not look like me. I had a wider nose with no curves on my body. My skin was lighter and darker than some girls. My lips are big and thick, and my hair has a mind of its own. I love all of it with all my heart. I truly do, but sometimes when my hair does not come out the way I want it to, it is aggravating. Sometimes I think about the forced diversity in some pageants. *Either I win because I am black, or I lose because I am black.* The thought is there because I must work for my opportunities. I had to learn how to say yes and step out of my comfort zone. I had to walk into troubling waters filled with animals of hatred, just to get opportunities I have never seen.

I was not expecting to win. I will be crowned Queen of my county in late 2020. Just a little bit more queen duties added to my plate. Even though I steered away from my original path for a while I have some great things to put on a college application. I still aspire to be a human rights lawyer and I still want to attend Howard University.

I know who I am now. I am a future Human Rights Attorney. I am a student attending Early College, who is about to begin their full college schedule of classes. I am a girl who loves her broad nose and smile. I am Miss Congeniality. I still fear failure. I am a girl who still fears being turned down. Pageantry has taught me to trust myself even when I am afraid.

Pageantry has also taught me that there is more than one path to success and sometimes it's the most undesirable path that in the end gets you to your destination.

Chapter 14
DREAMS THEY DO COME TRUE
ELYSE FAITH WOODSON

"In a world where you can be anybody and anything be bold, be fierce, be you, BeYOUtiful"
~Elyse Woodson

Dreams...They do come true!

Be bold, be fierce, be-YOU-tiful is the motto that I, Elyse Faith Woodson, live by. I am your 2018 National American Miss North Carolina Jr Pre-Teen Queen and Little Miss October 2018 Photogenic Miss.

For me, pageantry is not about beauty. I only compete in all-natural pageant systems that focus on self-confidence, inner beauty, and instill valuable lifelong skills. There is so much more to pageantry than just beauty. I am more poised, graceful, and stand prouder than before. Through the interview process of pageantry, I have learned to effectively communicate. I have developed public speaking skills from the personal introduction portion. The best part is I have created priceless memories and gained lifelong friendships. In fact, I met two close friends, Madison and Jiada. In the pageant world we call them sister queens and I met my BFF Trinity through pageantry. The runway is my absolute favorite pageant optional competition. I love fashion and I get to strut my stuff, show off my confidence and outfit, and let my personality shine.

It takes a lot of courage and self-confidence to stand on a stage and talk in front of large crowds of strangers. I balance it all by believing in myself, practicing a lot, and having patience with myself. My support system helps me balance it all too. They pray for me, encourage me, and believe in me. My superpower is being myself. In a world where you can be anything, I choose to be me, that is something nobody else can be. Pageantry helps me show the world that it's ok to be yourself. I believe there is nothing more beautiful than being you and loving yourself. My mom says people are drawn to me because I am myself and I am kind to everyone. I hope to encourage and motivate other young girls to shine bright, believe in themselves, be proud of who they are and love the skin they are in.

As a very outgoing, extroverted person, I enjoy meeting new people. Pageantry has helped me connect with other like-minded people and I am grateful for the bonds created. I want to inspire others to feel good about themselves from the inside out. I want them to know it is okay to be yourself. Being yourself means being authentic and real. If everyone embraced being themselves, I think the world would be a better and happier place. I want the world to know that your differences make you unique, special, and beautiful flaws and all!

One of the most rewarding parts of pageantry is doing volunteer work. I love helping others and giving back. I volunteered at as many places as I could. A Chance to Dance with Mrs. Kim at Mrs. Donna's School of Dance was my favorite place to volunteer. Here I received two bronze presidential volunteer service awards. For me, this is one of the best parts of pageantry.

My pageantry journey began in 2016 at the age of 6 years old when my mom received an invitation in the mail to the National American Miss North Carolina state pageant open call. We knew nothing about pageants, but my mom liked the fact that the pageant was natural, and I liked to sing and dance so we went to an open call where I was interviewed. A couple of days later I received a call back saying I was selected as a state finalist to compete in the pageant. I was nervous but excited.

We started preparing for the pageant by learning the pageant details and what it consisted of. There were six age divisions. My age division was princess, ages 4-6 years old. There were three required parts of the competition: formal wear, interview, and personal introduction. Formal wear is my favorite required competition. I felt so beautiful in my coral Tiffany Princess ball gown. During formal wear, every contestant is individually introduced on stage with their escort. You get to show off your dress of choice, your poise, grace, and confidence.

For the interview portion, there are seven judges that ask you different questions. You have up to one minute with each judge. The personal introduction is a 30-second speech talking about yourself, your dreams, and your aspirations. There were also optional contests. Since I consider myself a fashionista, competing in the casual wear competition was a must! My casual wear outfit was a leopard print romper with a pink flower belt and a pair of gold flats.

We traveled to Winston Salem, North Carolina for the pageant. It was held at the Benton Convention Center. With no experience, training, and little to no practice, I placed 3rd runner up overall in queens princess court, 1st runner up in the casual wear modeling competition, and I won the award for the most promising model! I was in complete shock and so happy that I cried for most of the night.

Because I placed top 5 in the queen's court, I received a golden ticket to go to Nationals in California. I experienced my first airplane ride and boy was I terrified but I conquered my fear of flying. As Miss Charlotte, I went to the happiest place on earth, Disneyland, toured Rodeo Drive, and took pictures in front of the

Hollywood sign with some of my new friends. While rehearsing the opening number production dance my dad won the spirit stick. It was great fun. At Nationals I competed in the talent, casual wear, and runway optional competitions. It was the experience of a lifetime and I will forever cherish the priceless memories created.

I enjoyed the state and national pageant so much I decided I wanted to compete again. My mom always tells me I can do anything I put my mind to and this time I wanted to win the title. My mind was made up to win. In 2018 I competed in a local pageant placing 1st runner up. My parents found me a pageant coach to help perfect my craft. I will forever be thankful for Mrs. Donna Murrell because she always believed in me.

In June we traveled back to Winston Salem to compete again. This time I competed in all the optional competitions, talent, actress, casual wear, photogenic, and top model photoshoot. I wore a yellow custom ball gown and my favorite Uncle Jeffery was my escort. I had the most fun ever this time. It did not matter whether I was crowned or not I was just grateful for the memories. The night of the finale I was a ball of nerves. I won the Spirit of America award, Miss Personality award, 2nd runner up casual wear, Miss Spirit 1st runner up, top model winner, best resume winner, 2nd runner up in talent, 1st runner up in actress, and I was the winner of the get acquainted/pajama dance-off.

I was elated to have won those awards, but nothing compared to getting my rose for top 10. They announced the South Carolina winner first. I was already crying because my friend Jiada won the South Carolina Jr. Pre-teen Queen title. When I heard them say, "your 2018 Miss North Carolina Jr. Pre-teen Queen is Elyse Woodson!" All I could hear was everyone screaming. It seemed like time froze. I remember looking out in the crowd at my mom, Yah-Yah, granny, and my sister. My mom was trying to jump up and down with a broken foot, my Yah-Yah dropped her iPad, she was so excited, and my granny was running around in a circle bursting with excitement. All I could do was cry and it was an ugly cry. I still get teased about my ugly cry, but it was well worth it as it was the happiest day of my life. My dream came true! I went to Nationals again where I won Miss personality and Miss Spirit award. I had an amazing year of reign.

Pageantry has afforded me so many opportunities. I was able to meet the mayor of Mecklenburg County, Miss Vi Lyles, and Cabarrus County mayor, Mr. William Dusch. I also received a congratulations letter from Congresswoman Alma Adams. I have had vocal training and artist development with J Stylz of Grammy award-winning R&B group, Blackstreet. I made my national television debut doing montages for ABCs Kids Say the Darndest Things. I have modeled in several fashion shows. I have been trained at Miss Donna's School of Dance in competitive jazz, tap, hip hop, ballet, and lyrical dancing. I have been in two parades. I

Dreams They Do Come True

have been in the newspaper and I have my own spread in a magazine. I am now attending Barbizon, the top modeling and acting school. I will travel to Orlando in August to represent Barbizon at the Passport to Discovery scouting competition.

The key to being successful in life is believing in yourself and pageantry has helped me do just that!

Road to the Crown with Trinity Bush

Chapter 15
UNIQUELY ME!
SOPHIA SANDERS

*"There are so many things I could be...
but I want to be uniquely me and
continue to fight for equality."*
~Sophia Sanders

Being uniquely me. This is something I live by and always encourage others to do as well.

Growing up in a family of 8 can be hard at times. I dream of the day where I will get to have my own room! On the bright side of things, growing up in a big diverse family lets me be uniquely me and that's something I embrace and love. I am a middle child and the perfect blend of two cultures. A true Oregon girl, I love the fact that we get to experience all of the seasons here. I especially like summer because I love swimming at my grandpa's house. My life is always on the go and there isn't a ton of downtime between myself and 5 siblings. We really keep our parents busy.

One of the many things I keep my parents busy with is my passion for pageantry. When I first started pageants I was a baby and don't really remember, but the pictures sure are cute. My mom received an application in the mail and thought it looked fun. She liked that the pageant was all-natural and nothing like the pageants on TV. I did that one pageant as a baby and then didn't do another for a couple of years.

As a really little girl, pageants were something I liked to do for fun, and loved seeing my family cheer me on. I also really loved making new friends and of course I enjoyed the hotel swimming pools. Now, I really like feeling fancy in my big dresses on stage and traveling to different states which usually includes family road trips. Once we drove from Oregon to Florida across the country for an event, it was an amazing adventure. This shows just how dedicated my parents are to help us reach our goals and dreams.

I really loved when my grandma would make me themed pageant outfits! She once made me the cutest peacock outfit. The beautifully colored feathers stuck straight up out of the backside. Another time she made me an Autism awareness outfit for a benefit pageant. That was very close to my heart as my cousin has autism. My mom has a few of those special outfits put away in some bins for me to keep. Doing pageants, especially benefit pageants, has allowed me to help so much around my community. I have enjoyed helping raise money for the autism foundation, serving food at the local missions here in Portland, and even making sack lunches and going out as a family to serve. I have also enjoyed donating books and school supplies to my local elementary schools. I really like sharing posts on my Sanders Sisters page about my community service, hoping to encourage others.

Going to my first National pageant was a blast! Community service is one of the main requirements to participate in this pageant and this actually made me want to do this pageant even more, knowing they also found the importance of giving back to the community.

I had fun rooming with one of my best friends. I prepared with my amazing coaches and had been looking forward to the experience. I was only six years old so my mom picked out some cute outfits. I loved my emerald green gown and I felt pretty. That year at Nationals was really fun, I won prize money and a plaque for one of the best "Thank You" letters. I made lots of new friends, one of whom I am really close to still and I definitely learned how much work and how much fun a big National pageant is. I didn't place in the top 12 and I was disappointed because I knew something was missing, something that hid my sparkle and shine that year.

As I have gotten older, pageants have a different meaning to me. At almost every pageant I have attended I am approached and asked "where did you get that gorgeous curly red hair?" I usually respond with "my mommy and daddy" and if that still puzzles them my mom, usually with her funny face says, "from God". Over time, I began to realize just how different and unique I was. Did you know that only 5% of the world has red hair and blue eyes? It's super rare. So imagine that, and then add in the factor that my father is African American. I'd imagine that percentage is even lower and rarer. I also began to learn that a lot of people, even people in the pageant world, need to know and understand that being unique is amazing. Being unique should be celebrated and talked about more. I do not look like a lot of pageant girls around me. Sure some have red hair but they don't have my wide nose and usually never have the naturally curly hair I got from my dad. I have learned to embrace and rock my naturally curly hair on stage and feel proud of my differences. I have even learned to embrace when people ask about my hair or when people stare at me walking with my daddy because my differences have made me find that sparkle and shine that had been missing.

When I was 8 years old I decided I was ready to go back to Nationals again. This time a little older, a lot more confident in who I am, and ready to go all in. That year at Nationals was really special because my little sister also was doing the pageant. We worked really, really hard to get to Nationals.

Uniquely Me!

We did a few raffles and we also turned in pop cans (a LOT of pop cans) to help raise money for the costs. You know the saying "work hard, play hard" yep that's a saying my coach and parents say often to me. Going into Nationals that year felt different. I felt my purpose, I felt my uniqueness and I loved it. I worked hard with my coaches and worked hard at being the best me. I decided this year to talk more about exactly what makes me unique and what makes me different. In my introduction, I talked about wanting to be the first African American female President and how I am the perfect blend of my African American dad and Caucasian mother. I felt strong, empowered, and beautiful on stage doing my introduction. For Talent, I decided to recite a powerful poem about being a black child. I wore an African outfit that was yellow, green, and black and received many compliments on it which made me feel happy. I felt proud when a mom came up to me after my poem and let me know how thankful she was and how beautiful of a job I did. It felt good to be on stage openly and confidently talking about what makes me different and what makes me uniquely me. I felt so beautiful and powerful.

Right before going on stage for formal wear my dad and I did our secret handshake and that loosened me up a little bit. I was standing there really nervous, thinking about how hard I worked and "BAM" just like that I heard them call Oregon for the top 12. That has been the biggest shock of all my life so far. At that moment I felt proud, I felt alive and I felt 100% uniquely me and I am forever grateful the judges saw that. I also felt scared, nervous, and shocked!!! I didn't know that all my hard work, confidence, and self-love would really pay off this big!! I had seen others in the past make the top 12 but OMG, it happened to ME! As it was time for the top 12 to do their introductions again, let's just say I kinda froze until my mom yelled across the stage a few of my words from my introduction to remind me. Yep she's that mom!

I didn't make the top 5 BUT, I made the top 12 in the nation!!! I would have loved to give you the typical happy ending but I am giving you my unique happy ending and I can only go up from here. Sure I was sad for a little bit after but it was nothing that couldn't be fixed with a hug from my two besties! I feel it was all part of God's plan for me and I took so much away from the win, loss situation.

I started to realize that differences are things that are hard and scary for people to talk about. We all have differences and things that make us uniquely us, some can be seen and some can't but we all have them. Being on the pageant stage has given me a place to speak about diversity and equity and about being different and unique and embracing it, no matter what those differences are. Sure I can look at Nationals as another loss but I used my voice all week long to speak up about embracing people's uniqueness and differences and the importance of loving and accepting them. So really for me, I look at it as a big win! Embracing your uniqueness is something I am really passionate about along with helping in my community and posting positive affirmations about self-love. I am lucky enough to have family and friends that help support and educate me along my journey and I hope to do the same for others along the way.

I was once a girl who was a little bit shy and who lacked self-confidence but today have used the pageant stage to speak my truth and voice to let the world know that being different is what makes you beautiful.

My road to the crown will always be full of passion, faith, dedication, and most importantly always being uniquely me.

Road to the Crown with Trinity Bush

MEET THE AUTHORS

TRINITY BUSH

BEYOND WHAT YOU SEE

> www.BeyondWhatYouSee.net
>
> TrinityBush0715@gmail.com
>
> Facebook @TrinityBush15
>
> Instagram @TrinityBush15

Captivating, Empowering, and Strong. Trinity Bush is the 10-year-old powerhouse hailing from Charlotte, North Carolina.

Ever since Trinity was able to speak, she has been tantalizing and captivating the attention of those around her. Her larger-than-life personality and spunkiness are beautifully displayed each time she takes the pageant stage. Trinity holds many pageant titles and the ones she is most proud of are her 2018 Carolina Girls Rock Jr. Preteen and 2019 North Carolina Jr. Preteen titles.

As a busy 5th grader at Southlake Christian Academy, Trinity is a girl who loves to discover new things. She loves science, American sign language, writing, and reading!

Trinity is the true definition of well-roundedness. Not only is she a pageant princess, but she is also a skilled dancer, academically successful student, and money-making CEO. She is an Amazon Best Selling author, A/B Honor Roll student, recipient of the 2020 S.T.R.E.A.M. New Entrepreneur Award, and the Visionary Author of this powerful anthology.

Trinity uses her platform to speak to audiences about facing their fears and embracing self-confidence. Trinity is the founder and CEO of Beyond What You, LCC. The mission of Beyond What You See is to empower and inspire people to embrace their perfect imperfections, face their fears, and do it anyway. She wants people to look beyond what they see in the mirror to find their true inner strength. She accomplishes that mission as a keynote speaker, author, audio recording artist, and apparel designer.

Confidence doesn't come when you have all of the answers but it comes when you are ready to face all of the questions and Trinity is facing them all head-on.

Meet the Authors

TRINITY WOULD LIKE TO ACKNOWLEDGE.

Mommy, Daddy, Aunt Leisha, Granny Pat, Granddaddy, Granny Dulla, Granny Amanda, In Loving Memory of Uncle Ronnie Smith, Delcina Felder, Zhaniya "Inspires" McCullough, Trinity Pearson, Ramiyah Griffen, Your Sister Queen Cherokee Ramsey, Kaelyn Clark-Middleton, Cedric Blackwell, Aissata Bah, Trinity Pearson, Ramiyah Griffen, and Alivia Issac.

JAKSYN BROWN

CELEBRATE YOUR CROWN

www.jaksynbrown.com

jaksynbrown@gmail.com

Facebook: @jaksyn.brown.77

Instagram: @jaksynbrown

If you're ever fortunate enough to share an elevator ride several floors to your destination with Jaskyn Brown, get ready because she's never met a stranger. From an early age the witty, champion public speaker has had a gift for gab. Before she could talk, she communicated using sign language. At the age of three, she memorized and recited speeches for annual community events and when she was six, won her first oratorical competition with her motivational speech "Unleash Your Superpower" blossoming into a confident go-getter who is never afraid to speak her mind.

In addition to public speaking, Jaksyn is no stranger to the stage. The young actress and pre-professional ballerina has performed in countless dance competitions, talent shows, runway, and modeling competitions. She also snagged a principal role in a national shoe retailer commercial which is her most favorite to date.

Walking a mile in Jaksyn's shoes includes having one named after you. Her vibrant personality and steady involvement in the fashion and youth industries have caught the attention of several brands, including New York fashion designer, Marc Defang, where the lilac floral and laced "Jaksyn" shoe is giving little divas everywhere the ability to make a statement without saying a word.

With a heart to serve, Jaksyn has been awarded the Presidential Volunteer Service Award for outstanding accomplishments in her Texas community. Jaksyn is a dedicated servant who has raised funds for childhood cancer research, volunteered with the Chocolate MINT Foundation, and advocates for the elimination of hair discrimination in schools and the workplace by bringing attention to the Crown Act. Her latest social impact initiative is her project *Celebrate Your Crown*, which encourages self-love and acceptance.

In the future, she aspires to become a plastic surgeon. For now, she's living a fun-filled life as a "daddy's girl" testing her limit on sweet confections from her favorite candy shops.

JAKSYN WOULD LIKE TO ACKNOWLEDGE.

Clarence and Amber Brown, Addison Wells, Myra McKinney, Sametria Netsanet, Dr. Charmeka Lipscomb, Jasmine Punch, Nayla Collins and the Collins Family, Rylie Teeter, Mia Bella Wilson, Kai Davis, Sarah Cooper, Alyssa Dass, Tayah Allen, Taylor Small, Abigail Maiden, Kendra Hale, Lilly Fauci, Barbara and Andre Punch, Linda Morgan and Brenda Roberson.

LACI ELLA BROWN
LACI'S HUNGER GAMES

LaciEllaOfficial@gmail.com

Facebook: @laciella.brown

Instagram: @laciellaofficial

"Though she be but little, she is fierce." When Shakespeare penned these words, he had Laci Ella Brown in mind. Laci is a 12-year-old powerhouse who came into the world as a 3lb 14oz preemie and has since been a force to be reckoned with.

Hailing from Lee's Summit, Missouri, Laci began public speaking at the age of 2 years old. Her captivating personality led her to begin participating in pageants at age seven where she won her very first title. Laci has continued with pageantry and has won numerous titles, accolades, and opportunities.

As a community activist, Laci has raised over $580 for a local community food network and she dedicates her time to stocking outside food pantries near neighborhood elementary schools. She established Laci's Hunger Games as a way of challenging her family and friends to bring awareness to and help end food insecurity for the children in her community.

Laci is an author and talented musician. As a musician, she is currently mastering the piano, violin, and ukulele. She is also a skilled vocalist debuting on a collaboration CD covering "Count on Me" by Bruno Mars. Laci's other interests include acting and modeling. She plays competitive volleyball and swims in a competitive summer league. Her favorite thing to do with her free time is abstract and landscape paintings on canvas.

Laci loves the Lord and her faith and spirituality are very important to her. She was baptized at the age of 10 years old and participates in the Children's Choir and on the Praise Dance Team at her church. She enjoys watching blockbuster movies and traveling with her parents. Her favorite vacation spots are Punta Cana and Puerto Rico. Most importantly, Laci loves hanging out with her friends and just being a preteen kid.

Laci is a proud member of Jack and Jill of America Inc, Girl Scouts of America, and Suburban Balance.

Meet the Authors

LACI WOULD LIKE TO ACKNOWLEDGE.

Mommy & Daddy, Grandma Ella & PawPaw Oree, Granny Laureen & Grandpa Larry, Uncle JR, Nana Delores & Papa Fields, Schardae Dupriest, Nicole Knop, Aunt Connie & Kim, Aunt Glo, Constance & Amber Crossley, Ms Kelli Lassman, Aunt Pamela Beasley, Laila and Chondra Walters, Sandra & Jordan McKinney, Auntie Tiffany & Parker, Auntie Carla & Kennedy, Sophia MacInnis, Aunt Lezona Williams, Auntie Claudette Holt, Skylar & Makayla Watson, Aunt Angela & Uncle Mario.

JURNEE ELYSE BUSH

SQUEEZE THE JUICE LEMONADE

www.SqueezeTheJuiceLemonadeCLT.com

SqueezeTheJuice27@gmail.com

Facebook @SqueezeTheJuiceLemonade

Strong, Brave, Avid reader, and Introverted extrovert. These are just a few of the words that describe Jurnee Elyse Bush. Jurnee is an 8-year-old well-rounded kid from Charlotte, North Carolina.

Jurnee is a busy 3rd grader who runs a unique business making and selling her own freshly squeezed lemonade, a level 3 gymnast who loves to flip and move her body, and a loving kid who deeply loves her sisters.

Jurnee is the youngest sister of 3. Being the youngest sister brings some interesting life experiences. For many years her sisters would talk for her and do things for her. Jurnee was indeed the

Meet the Authors

baby of the family and was spoiled even by her parents and grandparents. Jurnee's already introverted personality was becoming stronger. Jurnee decided it was time to break out of her shell and become MORE of herself. Jurnee put aside her lemonade apron and leotard and tried her hand at something new. Jurnee grabbed a small heel, ballroom gown, and headed to the pageant stage!

Jurnee competed for 2 years at the Carolina Girls Rock Pageant. She is the reigning 2019 Carolina Girls Rock Princess. The pageant world brought out her inner extrovert. Jurnee began to blossom verbally and was talking more than ever as a result of having to use her verbal skills to compete in pageants.

Jurnee is a girl on fire! She is a girl that runs a business, she is a girl that is growing in her gymnastic abilities, she is a girl that loves the pageant stage, she is a girl that is ready to run the world!

JURNEE WOULD LIKE TO ACKNOWLEDGE.

Mommy, Daddy, Aunt Leisha, Granny Pat, Granddaddy, Big Sissy Kylah, Granny Dulla, Granny Amanda, In Loving Memory of Uncle Ronnie Smith, Olive Wise, Taylor Medlin, Aniyah & Aliyah Oakley, Cousin Jaidynn, Cousins Xavier & Caileb, Cedric BlackwellUncle Ronnie Smith, Olive Wise, Taylor Medlin, Aniyah & Aliyah Oakley, Cousin Jaidynn, Cousins Xavier & Caileb and Cedric Blackwell

REAGHAN DANEE

Reaghandanee@gmail.com

Instagram @reaghandanee

Be Bold, Be Brave, Be Courageous, BE YOU.

Reaghan Danee is a ten-year-old model who is uniquely bold, uniquely brave, and completely confident in everything that makes her special. Born in Dallas, Texas, her big personality is perfectly accentuated by her big dreams and big goals.

Lover of high fashion and dressing-up, Reaghan began her modeling career as a print model for several magazines such as Child & Family, Beyond the Moon Lifestyle, Hitech, and A' LA Mode Child-Teen. When Reaghan dresses up, she feels fierce, powerful, and confident. When she takes the stage you can see she not only feels those things she embodies them as well

Meet the Authors

As a gymnast, actor, cheerleader, and soccer player, Reagan knows and understands the value of teamwork, the benefits of living a healthy lifestyle, and the fact that real happiness doesn't come from winning a medal but through the lessons learned along the way. As a straight-A student recently diagnosed with dyslexia, Reaghan continues to prove that there is nothing she can not do.

After losing her grandmother to breast cancer five years ago, Reaghan became a strong activist and philanthropist, passionately volunteering for the Susan G. Komen Foundation. Reaghan uses her platform to educate others about breast cancer awareness, the importance of early detection, and the importance of funding cancer research.

Reaghan believes in living life with passion and conviction. Her commitment to "living her best life" is what makes Reaghan a truly bright star.

REAGHAN WOULD LIKE TO ACKNOWLEDGE.

In loving memory of Nana (Sophronia Wilson), Dr.Dominique Wilson, Dr. Woodrow and Julia Wilson, Dr. Davonna and Brenda, Dylann Wilson, Derrick and Arvel Pride, Believe Pageant Consulting, Yordanos Melake, Angela Yates Webber, Kevin & Marian & Lexi & Krisi Gardner, Jessica Jones, Wanda Washington, Sharron Scott, Anita Nichols, Toni Jones, Mr. Larry and Dr. Janelle &Quin Shnoster, Ryan Thornton, Lynda Carmouche, Murray & Ruth Jones, Jackie Veal and Dienasti Reign.

CLORIESA KEITH DARDEN
KEITH'S EUNOIA

clokeith@icloud.com

Instagram: @cl0riesa

My name is Cloriesa Darden. I am a fifteen-year-old student who currently attends Onslow Early College in Jacksonville, North Carolina. I am a 2019-2020 Queen, a third runner-up in a state pageant, the 2020-2021 Miss Teen of Onslow County, and a current contestant in a Jabberwock Pageant.

I was born in Meriden, Connecticut, and soon moved down to North Carolina when I was a baby. Until I was four years old, I lived with my mother and my grandmother, also known as Nana. My mother and my Nana have and still are making an influential impact in my life. They both have taught me to be strong; there is no limit to my dreams. They have also taught me the reality of life and how I can overcome any obstacles that come my way.

When my mother had gotten married to my step-father new opportunities were thrown my way. I had my family had grown and I was introduced to great people. I had started basketball in third grade and had put my long legs to use. Though my dream was always to be a model and help my community. After the devasting hurricane in 2018, in Hurricane Florence, I had quit basketball. After, I was more focused on building my model career. And my mother supported me all the way.

Towards the end of 2018, my mother suggested a pageant in Charolette. I did want to do pageants because I was not a "girly girl," but I said yes anyway. Later, I realized pageants were not about beauty and who supported you. I had the greatest support and I was always intelligent; I also had the awards, but I need more service hours. I had taken my fifth-grade service project and turned it into a community-wide service. I am the founder and leader of the Blanket Ministries.

For pageants, you had to have a passion. I had pinpointed my passion for helping people who were betrayed by the system or who cannot fight for themselves. As a feminist and social activist, I was and still am using my voice to speak for others who cannot speak for themselves. I had created the blanket ministries to give help and comfort to people in need. I buy and collect blankets, wash them, and give them away with care packages, to people who are laid on my heart. Since 2019, I have had the primary focus of donating my collected items and care packages to the women's shelter.

In the states pageant, I had entered the category called spokesmodel. I had done this because I have always loved poetry and if you get me going, I can talk. At the pageant, I had spoken about Angelina Grimke and how allies such as her, helped people that looked like me. As a fifteen-year-old African American girl, I was always worried about something. I had gone through hardships; from the guilt of being on one side of colorism to being bullied because of my lips. I had used this as fuel during the Black Lives Matter movement in June. I had spoken against inequality before in my first pageant. But towards the end of May had used my platform and submitted an article talking about injustices in my country. My goal is to keep spreading public awareness about not only what is going on in my country but other countries too. It may not affect me directly, but I do have human compassion. I will help other minorities and ally with them. While knowing my passions I had also settled on the way to my future.

From the city of Jacksonville, North Carolina I am a future attorney for human rights. I am a 2023 graduate with my diploma and associate degree. I am a future student at Howard or Hampton or possibly Winston- Salem University. I will be the cool aunt who travels around the world to give people hope. I am a motivational speaker and the leader of the Blanket Ministries. I am Cloriesa Darden.

Road to the Crown with Trinity Bush

CLORIESA WOULD LIKE TO ACKNOWLEDGE.

Ma and Dad, Cousin Kyndra Brown, Uncle Perry Carr, Jesse "Big Brother" Davis, Echo Royal, Cousin Robin Dunn, Uncle Dean and Anutie Jennifer Hatcher and Family, Gloria "Nana" Anderson, Cousin Maison and Kasandra Hatcher, Cousin Madalyn Hudak, Aunt Noshima Darden-Tabb, The Darden Family, Grandma Janie Thrope, Lorriane Winston, Tina Winston-Green, Deacon Mike Fierce and Family, Usher Tania Fierce, Cousin Michelle Crane, Curtis and Tonya Hooks and Kubi Keyes.

CAYLEE AND ABIGAIL HAUCK
ABBY'S DESIGN BOUTIQUE ON ETSY

> https://twinsisterqueens.com
>
> Instagram @cayleeandabigail
>
> Facebook @shonsgirlly

Hello, We are Caylee and Abigail Hauck. We are twins who love to do pageants, ballet, jazz, and tap. We also love acrobatics and hip-hop dances. We are both in 2nd grade currently and will be moving to 3rd grade soon.

Caylee holds titles as 2020-2021 Miss Mecklenburg County Junior Preteen with National American Miss. She also won Top Photogenic with Miss Diamond Universe.

Abigail is currently the 2020-2021 Miss Charlotte Junior Preteen for National American Miss. She also holds the title of the Miss Diamond Universe Princess.

We both hold titles, Miss National Heart of America, since 2019. This is our third year. Abigail is the Miss Land of the Sky and Caylee is Miss old North state.

Though we are twins, we have separate interests at times which are few and far in between. We love doing things together as well.

Abigail wants to start her own business called Abby's Designs Boutique where she will sell her hand-crafted items. She loves anything to do with Arts and Crafts and loves handing them out to anyone. She wants to be a teacher when she grows up for Kindergarten. She loves school and volunteers by sending greeting cards to Senior Homes.

Caylee loves making her own games on her computer and sharing them with friends and family. She volunteers by baking goods for senior homes as well as helping her sister create greeting cards to send to Senior Homes. She loves school and learning that when she grows up she wants to be a teacher and school nurse.

Abigail and Caylee both are Read to Achieve Ambassadors, Kids Slime Club Ambassadors. Victoria's R. A. K ambassadors which are Random Acts of Kindness ambassadors.

They are both Rock Your Hair hair models and have their own hair care business with Rock Your Hair. They are also dance and cheer ambassadors. They are each part of the Role Models International. They stay busy and they love helping out in any way they can.

Meet the Authors

CAYLEE AND ABIGAIL
WOULD LIKE TO ACKNOWLEDGE.

Kendal Malone, Ipaye Family, Aunt Faye, Mommom,
Granny and Grandpa Hauck, General Steele,
Shon & Tracey Hauck, Smith family & Logan,
Aunt Nicole & Uncle Paul, Linda & Billy Bradford,
Charles & Debbie Ramos, Christina Bradford,
The Wallace Family, The Aklus Family, Zaylie Smith,
Loretta Hughbanks, Erin Montgomery, Ginger DeHaan,
The Roy Family, Jennifer McGugan

ABIGAIL HAUSER

www.RockinItwithKindness.com

Abigail.Hauser.official@gmail.com

Your voice is your superpower and finding your superpower is life-changing.

Abigail Hauser is a strong, beautiful, and charismatic preteen who discovered her voice at the age of three. While this was a bit later than some, her story of being completely nonverbal to becoming a verbal child who uses her voice for change is truly inspiring.

Born in Missouri, Abigail is the youngest of two girls and the daughter of a retired Army Major. She began participating in pageant competitions in 2015 and has loved every moment of it. One of the things she likes most about participating in pageants is the opportunity she has to make new friends.

Meet the Authors

Not only does Abigail love pageantry, but she is also a well-rounded student at Neil Armstrong Elementary School. She enjoys reading and she loves writing. As a 6th grade student, she participates in Spelling Bees, Mock Trials, Lego League, and Battle of the Books.

Abigail is also a philanthropist and community activist who is passionate about spreading kindness. She is the founder of *Rockin' It with Kindness*, an organization whose mission is to encourage kids across the country to make a positive difference in their communities.

When she isn't walking the runway or devouring a good book she loves to hang out with friends, build with Legos, and participate in Taekwondo. One of her favorite quotes is by Shakespeare, which says "Though she be but little, she is fierce" this quote is a perfect example of Abigail and her dynamic personality. It is also the quote that gave her the strength to conquer the final test on her journey to becoming a Taekwondo black belt.

In the future, Abigail plans to be a Veterinarian Chiropractor working with exotic animals and until then she is determined to make the world a better place to live.

ABIGAIL WOULD LIKE TO ACKNOWLEDGE.

Alyssa Jacob, Ashley Gruber, Shannon Corley,
Samantha Kissell, Tiffany (Coker) Hunt, Sydney Ruark,
Cathy Lockman, Jen Lockman, DeeAnn Schenk, Naomi Ochs,
DeeDee Salinas, Scott County Library System,
MaryJo Nelson, Echo Bennett, N.A. Elementary School,
Moeller Family, Laura Engle,
and most importantly - my mom & sister.

JAZEL BELLA JOHNSON

www.jazelbella.com

jazelbellajohnson@gmail.com

Instagram @jazelbella

Facebook @JazelBellaJohnson

She has a magic that is all her own. Her name is Jazel Bella Johnson.

Jazel Bella Johnson affectionately known as Jazel Bella is a 10-year-old pageant princess, model, dancer, community activist, and kid CEO. Her beautiful and charismatic personality has captured the hearts of people all over the world and has opened many doors of opportunity.

Jazel Bella participated in her first pageant in 2018. As a novice in the pageant world that year Jazel Bella represented the great state of Pennsylvania and was crowned *"Miss Philadelphia*

Jr. Pre-teen" a title she held for two consecutive years. In 2019, she won Miss Pennsylvania Jr. Pre-Teen Talent, Actress, Causal Modeling, and Most Promising Model along with numerous other awards and accolades. She won National Ambassador for 2018-2109 and 2019-2020. She also won a Miss Personality Award at the National pageant. Her charismatic and contagious personality is a sure contributor to her earning each of those crowns. Jazel Bella loves participating in pageants for many reasons but most of all she enjoys meeting new friends and having the opportunity to connect with people from all around the world.

In addition to being a natural beauty, Jazel Bella is also a brilliant student. As a current 5th grader, she is an honor roll student who speaks 3 languages and excels in language arts, science, and math. Jazel Bella is a star student who loves supporting her fellow classmates and always makes new students feel welcome with her warm and inclusive personality.

Not only is Jazel Bella a talented student, but she is also a Kid CEO who is very active in her community. In 2017 Jazel Bella and family launched the "J. Bella" brand and clothing company. Through her business, she hopes to inspire others, especially girls to love themselves and embrace their unique style. As a young CEO, she uses her platform and resources to serve her community by volunteering at the local nursing home, Rescue Mission homeless shelter, and local food bank.

Meet the Authors

In her spare time, Jazel Bella loves to play with her younger brother, participate in activities such as ballet, praise dancing, acrobatics, tap, hip-hop, tennis, basketball, chess club, and swimming. Jazel Bella has been featured as a guest on FOX 29 "Q Show". She also led the countdown and performed a dance solo at the District 9 Holiday Christmas Tree lighting.

In the future, Jazel Bella Johnson plans to be a world-famous designer and lawyer, but until then her focus is on making the world a better place to live, love, and shine.

JAZEL WOULD LIKE TO ACKNOWLEDGE.

Jamar (Dad) & Dr. Louisa (Mom) Johnson & Jamar Jr., GrandPa Gaiter, Grammy Johnson, GrandMa Sarah, GMAC Joyce, Uncle RaShawn, Daymond, Yasmeen & Christian, Auntie Regina & Jean Skeeters, Uncle Brenton, The Blain Family, Aunt Laurie & Family, Keem & Dom, Aunt Martha Douglas, Aunt Delores & Ruby Brooks, LaTonya & The Gaiter Family, Hassell Family, The Mills Family, Mrs. Brenda, Hawkins & Smith Families, Aunties Yandy Smith-Harris, Candie, Tika, Jeanelle, Chelsea' & Tashyra Ayers, John & Dr. Alesha Smith, The Spain Family, Jesse DeBerry, Earl Johnson, Geraldine Brown, Mrs. Norma & Ramona Wilcox.

CORTNEY LISBY

SWEET AND CHARMED

sweetandcharmedbycortney@gmail.com

Leader, Creator, World Changer.

At the age of 10 years old, Cortney Lisby is an award-winning pageant princess. As the 2017 National American Miss South Carolina Princess, Cortney is no stranger to standing out confidently, boldly, and beautifully.

Cortney is an active and academically successful 5th grader at Carolina Springs Elementary School where she excels in reading, writing, and physical education. As a member of the Leadership and Ambassador Club, Cortney's true heart of compassion and kindness is demonstrated as she welcomes newcomers to the school and extends friendship to anyone in need of a friend.

Meet the Authors

When Cortney is not dominating the pageant stage or leading her peers at school, you can find her making Tik Tok videos, perfecting her baking skills, or designing customized charm bracelets.

On or off the stage Cortney's positive attitude and a brilliant smile lights up any room. Her goals and ambitions are awe-inspiring and there is no doubt that she will accomplish them all. Cortney is committed to making an impact on the world, by ensuring that everything she does is done in excellence. Cortney may be small, but she has a big heart and at 10-years-old she is a beautiful, smart, and bold young lady who is already making big moves.

CORTNEY WOULD LIKE TO ACKNOWLEDGE.

Mom, Dad & Brothers, Eva & Johnny Burgess, Alex & KayK Bradley, Lisa Burkett, Lizzie Mae Harmon, Latoya Brockington, Linda Bartley, Marvie Quattlebaum, Charles Moultrie, Gloria Quattlebaum, Loretta Bookard, Stacey Razor, Pearl Billingslea, Angela Holmes, Calvin Quattlebaum, Marilyn Mingo, Todd Brown, Sandy Cherry, Tomeka Love, and Jessica Moyer.

PRINCESS PARIS NDU

PRINCESS PARIS GLOBAL

www.princessparisndu.com

Parisndu@yahoo.com

Facebook @billiondollarorincess

Never underestimate a dreamer for it is the dreamers who change the world. Paris Ndu is a dreamer and her dreams are as big as the world.

Born in Houston, Texas to Nigerian parents, Paris is a gifted six-year-old who has a passion for fashion and style. She began participating in pageant competitions in 2019 and holds many titles.

Not only does Paris have a radiant smile that can fill any room, but she also has a captivating personality. She is bright, tenacious, charismatic, and kind. One of the things she likes most about participating in pageants is the opportunity she has to make new friends which is something she is very good at doing.

Paris is the CEO of a children's clothing company whose mission is to clothe the world so no child has to live without clothes. She began this company to generate funds to contribute to charitable organizations that support children's education. Blessed with a heart to give, Paris donates 10% of every sale she makes to a charitable organization that encourages children to go and stay in school.

An excellent student, Paris excels in Reading, Math, and Science. She is currently a Read to Archive Program Ambassador where she joins a network of readers worldwide working to ensure that every young child who may not be read to at home, has someone to read to them. She is also an ambassador of International Read To me" where she also reads to children online.

While Paris is an only child, this doesn't stop her from entertaining herself with big dreams and endless possibilities. She enjoys imagining and dreaming, reading, illustrating, singing, and dancing. In the future, Paris plans to be a veterinarian but until then she is determined to make the world a better place to live.

PARIS WOULD LIKE TO ACKNOWLEDGE.

Mommy and Daddy, Carrie McMahon, Glo E.,
JaMaria Howard, Eleanor McMahon, Chloe Ivie Eke,
Julie Anyanwu, Ann Kutyna. Jayden Obiefuna, Ebele Udalor,
Ify Ibekwe, Nkiru Onwuemelie-Nwokike, Nkechi Ofondu,
Lady Onyi Ikebuaku, Lady Theresa Ezinwa,
Chief Osita Solomon Agu, Jacinta Ekweonu,
Adrian And Arya Parameswaran, Chibuzor Cyril Ezinwa
and Chineye Joy Agu.

JAZMINE VANESSA PALMA

lynnpalma@ymail.com

Hi, my name is Jazmine Palma, I am a 10-year-old who attends First Ward Creative Arts Academy. I am learning to speak Spanish and French. My father is from Guatemala and my mom is American. I was born In Pineville, North Carolina on my grandmother and Aunt's birthday. I also have 3 brothers and 1 sister. I am the baby and have my daddy wrapped around my fingers. I have visited Guatemala where my father's family is. It is a beautiful country with great people that live there. Seeing the countryside and trying different things was a great experience.

I have learned to read Spanish and speak some Spanish. I have been doing pageants since I was 5 years old, but only all-natural pageants. Learning what I have learned over the past 5 years has been more fun and useful in everyday life and my future. I have very big dreams to achieve like getting accepted into

Harvard law school and become a family law attorney or a sexual assault lawyer. I learned I want to be a lawyer because I have seen videos and movies about the way in which kids are abused and sexually assaulted. I want to learn how to get them justice or peace.

I love to shop, what girl doesn't. Me and my mom go shopping and looking for clothes or dresses for me, and I start thinking about my future, "When I become a lawyer, I will buy you the house of your dreams and the most beautiful dresses and we will live in Malibu." I love telling my mom this. I love watching videos on how to do makeup as a hobby and taking care of my dogs.

JAZMINE WOULD LIKE TO ACKNOWLEDGE.

Leslie Flores Cameros, Jasmine Cayetano, Nedra Tareen, Debbie Zambrano, LeAnn Peyron, Monica Nunez, Lynn Palma, Nichelle Nelson, Londyn M. and Maggie Barr

ZARIA MARTIN RILEY

www.zariamartinriley.com

zariamartinriley@gmail.com

FB: @ZariaMartinRiley

IG: @just_1zari

"Little girls with dreams become women with vision" Zaria Martin Riley is the dream manifesting, a vivaciously curious, and dynamically compassionate young woman who is taking the world by storm. Hailing from the great state of Maryland, Zaria is articulate, creative, and strong.

She began participating in pageants at the age of 6 and has participated in various pageants since that time. While Zaria has numerous awards and titles, the one she is most proud of is the 2019 Top Model. She loves being in pageants for many different reasons, but her favorite part is the opportunities she gets to engage in public speaking and meet new friends from all over the country.

Zaria is a very compassionate young lady. She regularly volunteers at local food banks, food centers, and farmers' markets. One of her greatest passions is establishing friendships. Zaria believes that every child deserves a friend and in 2019 she was deeply saddened to discover that she was too young to volunteer at the city children's hospital. She is excited to turn 14 so that she can begin to volunteer as a friend to play with and provide company to the hospitalized children at her local hospital.

As a bright and talented 3rd grader, Zaria is a girl who loves to write. She is a straight-A student who enjoys learning, writing, and asking questions. Zaria is a very well-rounded child. Not only is she a pageant princess, but she is also an experimental cook, academically successful student, and curious tinkerer who learns very quickly.

When Zaria is not volunteering, walking the runway, or studying hard she enjoys hanging out with her twin brother, playing with her dog, Mystery, and inventing new hairstyles or recipes. In the future, Zaria plans to be a fashion designer, but until then her focus is on encouraging others, being a good friend, and filling the world with love and compassion.

Meet the Authors

ZARIA WOULD LIKE TO ACKNOWLEDGE.

Mommy & Daddy, Mrs. Teresa Cross, Mrs. Lynetta Dorsey, Auntie Nidda, Aunt Kiki, Mrs. Chari Christie, Auntie Ebony, Beverly "Bubba" Riley, Mrs. Zohnette Sligh, Mrs. Ida Britton, Avery & Harper, Aunties Marlene, Marilyn & Dedra, Ms. Saran Fossett, Godmommy Tanika, Godmommy Titania, Mr. Mark Dove, Mrs. Maya Henderson, Randy "Cave" Harris, Ms. Christina Garrett and Ms. Sharae Foreman.

SOPHIA AUDREY-JEAN SANDERS

simplythesanders.com

SophiaSanders0307@gmail.com

Facebook @SophiaSanders0307

Facebook @simplythesanders8

Facebook @sanderskids

Sophia Audrey-Jean Sanders came into this world making a big statement at 9lbs 12oz and a full head of bright red hair on March 7, 2012. From the beautiful state of Oregon, she's a girl who loves to go on family hikes and take day trips to the nearby ocean. Making a big statement has continued to be something Sophia lives by. She has big plans to become the first African American female President of the United States. Her backup plan is to become a Pediatric surgeon… like the saying goes "Shoot for the **moon**. Even if you miss, you'll **land** among the **stars**."

Meet the Authors

Sophia also known as Sophie by most has a passion for giving back in her community she believes no matter what your age is there are always ways to get involved. Although her crown and banner have given her amazing opportunities she believes you don't need a title to make a difference in the world. She has a passion for making sure children have school supplies and that everyone has a full belly and no one goes to bed hungry. Her large diverse family of 8 often shocks the world and has helped her realize the importance of being an advocate for self-love, and accepting your uniqueness. She found the pageant stage has helped give her a place to speak and educate others about the importance of diversity and acceptance of people's differences. She believes God made us all just the way we are supposed to be and as she always says "I am just being uniquely me".

Sophia's favorite food is Spaghetti and avocados. Her favorite color is pink so it makes sense that her favorite animal is a Flamingo. She thinks it's cool how a flamingo balances on one leg for so long. It is much like life, a constant balancing act. Speaking of balancing, this 3rd-grade student balances many things in her busy life. She is often the classroom helper and has been selected student of the month by her teachers several times. She is an A student and one of the selected few for the Talented and Gifted Program in her school. She really loves learning new things and loves being challenged. She enjoys reading a good chapter book and often writes in her journal.

Along with her passion for pageants, she also enjoys gymnastics, ballet, basketball, and soccer along with learning how to do her naturally curly hair and playing with her dolls. She enjoys modeling and acting and hopes to do more of that in the near future. She has a good hand at doing art especially drawing and is an excellent swimmer. She is a real mommy's helper and a true daddy's girl.

Sophia hopes that readers are left with inspiration to also make a big statement by truly embracing and taking the time to understand others' differences along with accepting and loving the things that make you unique. In a world where you can be anything, be uniquely you!

SOPHIA WOULD LIKE TO ACKNOWLEDGE.

Jabari & Jenny (Dad & Mom) & Jaiden & Sebastian & Jaslin & Savannah & Jabari (My Siblings), Grandma Audrey & Aunt Brittnee, Granny Delores & Grandpa Ernie, Grandma Sarah & Grandpa Curt, Tia Katie & Tio Guadalupe, Uncle Dustin & Aunt Jamie, Cousin Crystal & Daniel & Cousin Ashlee, Uncle Caine & Jason, Aunt Lynn, Aguirre Family, Believe Consulting & Photography, Lucrecia Carter, Maricella Charles, Kaylinn Hoyt & Charity Ramirez, Nicole Clayton, Nichole Baker, Jennifer Peterson, Heather Pascua, Tiffany Clark, Sade Rivers and Rikki Drews.

ALEXANDRA WILCOX

ALLIE'S BOOKS FOR CULTURES

www.alliesbooksforcultures.org

Instagram and TikTok @thealliealexandra

allieyaxinwilcox@gmail.com

Alexandra "Allie" Wilcox is the golden girl of Golden Valley, Minnesota, and her personality really shines when she gets to share her talents with a crowd. In addition to public speaking through pageantry, she has loved using her voice to teach others about her Chinese heritage and the cultural importance of Chinese New Year. Of course, using her voice has helped by the fact that she is fluent in two languages—English and Chinese—and she's getting pretty good in Spanish too, which she studies in school. Allie has always loved giving musical performances, from church choir when she was younger to piano performances in recitals and in her chapel at school.

Her love of music also plays a key role in her Latin dance and figure skating performances, and she has won multiple first-place awards in both types of competitions, with grace and flair that definitely gets noticed by the judges. Golden girl Allie is also a gold medal winner in chess, where her opponents quickly learn to fear this pageant queen's gambits.

Allie's love of performances and competitions is matched by her love of reading. Ever since she stunned her parents by suddenly reading restaurant menus to them at three years old, she has been a voracious reader. Whether it's C.S. Lewis, the encyclopedia, dragon stories, adventure stories, fantasy books, joke books, the Bible, or even economics books, Allie dives into them, is engrossed by them, and goes through them at record speed. There's a reason her teacher has referred to Allie as "the class Google"; she reads about everything, and when she reads about something she retains it.

In connection with her love of books, Allie is currently developing a cultural literacy program called Allie's Books for Cultures ("ABC"), with the hopes of raising kids' awareness of cultural diversity while promoting reading and literacy. Allie excels in every subject at school and loves learning; she would go to school seven days a week if they would let her. Allie loves to travel and has a great time visiting the lands of her ancestors (China, Iceland, and Canada) and on trips across the United States. Allie enjoys modeling and acting and hopes to do more of both in the future, and in the long term wants to be a professional photographer. Allie has competed in multiple pageants and has enjoyed building friendships and connections along the way. She is the 2021 International Junior Miss Minnesota Jr. Pre-Teen. She's also won Best Actress, Best Spokesmodel, and Best Resume at the state level.

ALEXANDRA WOULD LIKE TO ACKNOWLEDGE.

In loving memory of Grandpa Ken, and with special thanks to Grandma Norma, Grandparents Suxing & Anguo, mom & dad, Auntie Cindy, Chris & Caeli, Auntie Brenda & Uncle Mark, Grant & Kara Wilcox, Cindy Doolittle, the Kimbro family, Dr. Marti Erickson, the Lin family, Confidence & Poise, Ms. Wang, Auntie Yanling, Auntie Weijum, Lan Cao, Lee Rucker, Madeleine Johnson, Naiima Harrell, Ava Mehta, Teagan Miller, Hannah Simon, Emma & Ella Xia, Emma Yu, Lilyana Zanesco, Ella & Dingyu Zheng

ELYSE FAITH WOODSON

ElyseFWoodson@gmail.com

Facebook@elyse.woodson.1

Be bold, Be fierce, Be -YOU-tiful.

This is a powerful mantra by a powerful young lady. Elyse Faith Woodson is a 12-year-old North Carolina native who is taking the world by storm and making an enormous impact through her community activism, her academic excellence, and her love for pageantry.

Elyse has been participating in pageants since 2016. She has many titles but the title of which she is most proud is 2018 North Carolina Jr. Preteen. Elyse loves pageantry for many reasons. She loves meeting new people and making new friends, she enjoys speaking on stage, and she especially loves the fact that she can allow her personality and natural beauty to shine.

While Elyse loves participating in pageants she also loves school. As a straight "A" 6th grade student, Elyse demonstrates academic excellence in English, Reading, and History. She is a leader in her classes and helps with supporting students who need additional help with their class assignments.

Elyse is a confident preteen who believes in service. She is very active in her community and spends much of her time volunteering at local food banks and Habitat for Humanity. She also raises funds to support organizations such as the Breast Cancer Foundation and the Ronald McDonald house. One of the experiences dearest to her heart is her work with Chance to Dance. This is an organization that allows individuals with disabilities to experience dance while mentors like herself support them through the moves.

In her spare time, Elyse likes to dance, sing, play with her friends and care for her grandmother's dog Barkley. She is a young lady with many gifts, talents, and aspirations. She has big dreams and big goals and with her dynamic personality, they are all certain to come true.

ELYSE WOULD LIKE TO ACKNOWLEDGE.

Mommy & Daddy, Yah-Yah, Granny, Paw-Paw & Ma-Ma,
Reginald & Queserie Peay, PJ & Marlina Thompson,
Judah Ragin, Pauline Crook, Bridgette Thomas,
Dee Woodson, Yvette Stark, Ramona Collins, Natatiyah May,
Chemise Legette, Kisha Mims, Lena Jordan, Donna Murrell,
In loving memory of Leonard Barrier, Baron Massey,
and Ericka Springs.

www.ingramcontent.com/pod-product-compliance
Lightning Source LLC
Chambersburg PA
CBHW070904080526
44589CB00013B/1178